THE MAKING OF AN EVANGELIST

A Warrior Emerging
Through the Process of Transformation

Evangelist C. Maria Jones

innovo
PUBLISHING

Published by
Innovo Publishing, LLC
www.innovopublishing.com
1-888-546-2111

Providing Full-Service Publishing Services for
Christian Authors, Artists & Organizations: Hardbacks, Paperbacks,
eBooks, Audiobooks, Music & Film

THE MAKING OF AN EVANGELIST
A Warrior Emerging Through the Process of Transformation

Scripture quotes taken from the King James Version of the Holy Bible.

ISBN 13: 978-1-61314-237-0

Cover Design & Interior Layout: Innovo Publishing, LLC

Printed in the United States of America
U.S. Printing History

First Edition: September 2014

CONTENTS

DEDICATION

Dedicated to my God Who has nurtured and kept me through it all. Every hurt and pain He himself has borne for me so that I may be free. Free to love, to laugh, and to continue to learn by His grace and mercy. Lord, I am eternally in love with You. To all of my sisters near and far, I love and appreciate your hearts to endeavor through the struggles that this life offers us. As we move forward, we look up, for our redemption draws near. God bless you all.

SPECIAL ACKNOWLEDGMENT

A special thanks to my father, the late Willie Jones. It is because of his generosity this book is in circulation today. I love you.

PREFACE

This book is not about all the wonderful things that I have experienced in my life that would cause me to want to serve God. It is not about the preaching and teaching of the gospel. I am not writing to entertain you or to become known in this world. It is about when life meets the road to a destiny that you did not know existed. I have been offered mercy and grace through my Lord and Savior, Jesus the Christ. I am eternally grateful to Him.

So, I open the door of my life to extend divine grace to my hurting sisters that have not come out of the darkness of their pain. I share my pain that you may be set free. Many of my experiences are due to a divine destiny that was preset for me before the thought or act of conception had ever existed into the hearts of my parents. All of these things have worked together for the good. And in due season, the emergence of a true warrior will stand before you and declare what God has done.

Some of you may not believe there is an evil destructive force that is out to destroy our destinies. I speak not of the destiny that you may be creating. We can be led from our purpose when we are driven by greed, ego, manipulation, or when personal gratification is leading us. Our opinions, ideas, and plans can be good, but that does not mean they are of God. If we have not found our purpose in this life, rest and assurance of peace will not be possible.

The day will come when you will begin to ask and seek. You will begin to ask, *Why am I here? What is the purpose for my life?* If you seek long enough and are willing to go through the process of understanding the core of who you are, you will find your answers. You will begin to understand your uniqueness and embrace it. And you will understand the necessity of your uniqueness for where you are going.

God had a plan for my life from the beginning, and Satan had a plan to try to destroy it. We may or may not understand why some things happen to us. If we are willing to stay in the process, we will realize that God has been in it the entire time. Before you start thinking wrongly, I did not say God did it. I said that God was *in* it. He was in it to be with us as the strength that pulls us through. He is for us and not against us. I am quite sure that some of you can already attest to the devastation that has come into your life and rocked your world off its axis. If it had not been for purpose in your life, you probably would not be here today. But you are! That can only mean that you have not completed the destiny walk that is laid out before you. It is God's strength that sustains us so that in due season, we have a story that might be told and others might be strengthened. Then, our destinies are preserved and our suffering is not in vain.

We live in a nation of hurting people. Am I saying that everyone is hurting? No. But many don't understand the source of their dysfunction that they now call their "normal." We are reaping the consequences of the dysfunction of our forefathers and mothers. It is evident in our children and grandchildren's attitudes and behaviors. We cannot continue to close our eyes to the overwhelming destruction of sin that plagues our nation. I define *sin* as any act that eats away at the foundation of the family structure and value system according to the Word of God. Some sin we choose to walk into, and some sin we are born into. However it comes, it is there and we all have to deal with it. In the Holy Bible, David said, "I was shapen in iniquity," and so have we all in this life. By choice or by circumstance, we have got to face sin. Just remember that sin will take you farther than you want to go; it will keep you longer than you want to stay; and it will make you pay a price that you cannot afford.

It is my hope that as you read this book it will challenge you to search your heart in truth. I hope that it is encouraging, relatable, and prompts you to move forward. I believe this book will inspire you to reach toward healing and health to your mind, body, and spirit—they are all connected. One cannot function without the other in this life and be successful.

Focus on your destiny. Stop asking *why me* and learn to rise above the storms in your life. Be encouraged; change will come. No storm lasts forever. Amazing results will spring forth. When you go through the fire, it shall not burn you. Out of your ashes shall come the beauty of who you were always created to be. Old things must be torn away and replaced with the new. In the mist of the rebuilding process, you will not only find out who you are, you will find out Who the Almighty God is. Be prepared to be challenged. Be open to receive. And be hungry enough to seek truth. It shall be revealed.

> **"The spirit of the Lord God is upon me; because the Lord has anointed me to preach good tidings unto the meek; he has sent me to bind up the broken hearted, to proclaim liberty to the captives, and the opening of the prison to them that are bound; To proclaim the acceptable year of the Lord, and the day of vengeance of our God; to comfort all that mourn;" (Isaiah 61:1–2).**

CHAPTER 1

Things Are Not as They Suppose

Your destiny started before the crowning of your titles. It began even before those two chromosomes came together to become one. It started in the essence of God's glorious presence. It is the throne room of grace!

These accounts are taken from the words of my mother:

The late summer of 1964, my mother lost her second son. He was two years old and had been the only living son (her first was stillborn). At that time, she had four daughters. As with anyone who has lost a child, she was completely devastated. She had gone food shopping and had chosen to leave the younger children at home. She left the children with trusted, reliable family members. With the thought that all would be well, she went on her way. And when she returned, her child was dead. No one could explain what had happened and even the autopsy was unclear about the cause of death. Burdened with grief, guilt, hurt, and shame, my mother set her mind to conceive again. She thought that surely God would give her another son. My father was not in complete agreement with her. He felt that she had already had four children and did not need anymore. Only the youngest of the four daughters belonged to both my mother and father. *She must be crazy*, he thought. Having the one was enough for him. Although he lost his only son, he still had one girl. Needless to say, he gave into my mother's desire to conceive again, and I was born June of the following year.

In a small town in Central Florida, I was born in an all-white Catholic hospital. At that time in the South, women were still having their babies at home with the assistance of a midwife. Due to the special circumstances of my mother's pregnancy, it was recommended that she birth this baby in the hospital. The safety of her life and her child's life was at great risk. Having just lost a child the prior year, she wanted to take extra precaution. Even with that, there was no guarantee.

It was close to her due date and the baby had not turned into the birthing position; I was breech. That position is very dangerous for both mother and child. Most breech babies did not make it through natural birth in those days. It was likely that she would need surgery in order to deliver. Even today, the breech position is just as dangerous and requires surgery.

Her water broke and she went into labor. Her doctor received the call that she had arrived at the hospital. She was put in a room by herself to await his arrival. During those years, segregation was alive and kicking. As far as anyone else was concerned, she had no business even being there. As the doctor headed out to deliver his first black baby born in this all-white hospital, he fell and broke his foot. My mother was left to deliver her own baby.

Feeling the bearing pressure of the baby, the feet began to move down the birth canal. As the baby's feet started coming down, she lifted herself up and began to push. With this being the seventh child that she had given birth to, she was a bit of an expert in childbirth. As the feet began to emerge from out of the womb, she reached down and guided her baby out. Miraculously, she birthed a healthy baby girl into this world.

Although she anticipated the birth of a son, another daughter was given to her, and she was satisfied. After the birth, the nurses came in and cleaned her and her newborn up. When my father entered the room, he walked over to see the new edition to the family as I lay in my mother's arms. He was not happy that another daughter was brought into the family. With a few discouraging words, he walked away. In my mother's own words she said, "At that point, I knew I had to protect you."

You see, things are not always as they suppose. There can be much more to a story than what first meets the eyes. Some may see the tragedy in this story. I see the beginning of God's plan unfolding. When God has a plan for your life, there is no devil in hell that can stop it. My mother was looking for a son. God was working a plan. If we are willing to push through and stay on the path, destiny is bound to spring forth. I believe that when my mother lost her son she prayed to God for another son. In her heart, she told God that she would give this child back to Him. And God, in His infinite wisdom, said yes and chose me. What an awesome and wise God I serve! I could not die in the womb because purpose was calling me forth. I could not die in birthing because destiny was awaiting me. Even my birthing order spoke profoundly of the calling upon my life. The number seven is symbolic of completeness of God's work. I was the seventh pregnancy. I was the fifth living child. The number five represents a vow to the work of God and His favor and grace.

God had made promises to my forefathers and foremothers. God's Word cannot return to Him unfulfilled. His words must be complete and flourish in what He sent it to accomplish. My great-grandfather (my mother's grandfather) was a gospel preacher who travelled throughout the South carrying the Word of God. He was blind from birth, but it never stopped him from doing what he was called to do. He evangelized the lower Southern states and cared for his family and community.

I remember my mother telling me that they spent a large amount of time in church when they were younger. There is a scripture that says, "Train up a child in the way he should go: and when he is old, he will not depart from it" (Proverbs 22:6). This has been a proven fact in my mother's life as well as my own. Some of you may have grown up in church like I did. Be encouraged; if you have strayed off the path, you will find your way back.

There is usually one person around who people feel they can talk to and trust. In my great-grandfather's community, he was the one. He continually prayed for his offspring, even those he would never know. He spoke words of power and strength over them before they were ever born. He prayed that God would use them for His purpose and that He should be glorified through them. I never knew him, but I'm glad that he prayed.

My mother's loss was never a loss. It was a gain for her life and the kingdom of God. God allowed my brother to be taken. He used this evil and brought good out of it. He opened the door to my entrance into this world and into His purpose for my family and His kingdom.

The Silent Voice of My Mother

The life that once lived in my womb is now dead. This can't be so. No, not another. God help me! My baby is DEAD. All dread has gripped the soul of my being. I don't want to live through this. Help me to leave this sea of emotion that I am drowning in. Grief has swept over me like an angry sea fighting against the winds of heaven. Chaotic pain grips the perception of my reality in this world. Is anyone left in here? I have buried a part of myself in that deep, hollow, cold grave with my beautiful baby boy. I'm hurt and angry. My frustration is overtaking me.

The evil that this world has beheld for me is more than I can bear alone. One person should not have to carry this. Yet, I am. So much pain I'm suffering. So much pain I have endured. Agony overtakes me. Will it ever end? God, bring life back into me. I won't let it go again. I'm sorry! I promise You that I won't let it go again. Have mercy on my soul. Have mercy on my soul.

***

And with that, it would take almost forty years for my mother to stop punishing herself for the death of her son.

I don't know what it feels like to have lost a child. I am told that it is the worst grief that one could ever suffer. It's a grief that I don't want to know. I can't imagine the strength that it takes to bounce back from such a travesty. What I do know is that true healing comes from God and God alone. He is the only one Who can apply healing salve to an old or new wound. When true healing comes, the memory is not wiped away, but the pain of the experience no longer grips you with paralyzing thoughts. Tears become few and far between. Your conversations begin to come from a place of peace and love. It's a happy place, and a greater appreciation for life occurrences.

As a young child, I always remember my mother calling me her black Jesus. Hold off before you get too spiritual. It gave her peace, but it gave me great distress. I could not understand why she would always say this with a smile on her face. I never asked her to stop, although I always wished that it would be the last time she said it.

I was very dark skinned as a young girl. I was teased a lot about my color. Frequently, my color would be referred to with a contemptuous demeanor. This came from within the home more than outside of it. Children really do know how to be cruel, not realizing that their words can and do cripple character traits.

In the early seventies, black was not where it was at for me. People of color were beginning to identify with the greater mingling of diversity that had blended the Black American culture. The effects of division that slavery left on our people are almost irreversible. It has been in effect for so long that we have turned on ourselves. It is each of our responsibility to identify who we are as a whole and in truth. In our uniqueness, we have much to offer. In our unity, we can impact the world.

I had a lot of insecurities around this issue as I got older. So every time I heard those words—Black Jesus—I felt like she was pointing out flaws in my appearance that I had no control over. I thought, *Why do you keep putting me out there? You are my mother, but you are the one who keeps throwing me under the bus.* It took me a long time to understand what she was saying. In the midst of her darkest hour, God gave me to her to deliver her out of her own destruction. Her hope was gone. God's grace sent her deliverance unto salvation—my birth delivered her from depression.

The thoughts of a child, whether true or not, can lead to his own demise. A child's reasoning has not developed enough to process complex information. The results can be devastating. And destruction is the path it will take.

The vow that my mother made to protect me was a set up. We cannot protect our children from everything. No matter how much we are involved in our children's lives, life happens! The job that was before her was greater than she knew. She did not know that her best protection would be nowhere near enough for what the enemy had in store for me.

CHAPTER 2

The Early Years

I was almost two years old when my mother left Florida. My father and mother had a very physical relationship. My father would go out drinking and gambling on payday. When he would come home, he would be drunk, broke, and wanting to fight. My mother was 5' 2" and my father was 6' 6". My mother was short, but she was tough. She had no fear when it came to fighting. It became normal for her to call the cops almost every weekend.

One night after he came home from drinking and gambling, he took the food out of the freezer to sell in order to continue gambling. My mom had had enough. She went to her mother's house and gathered enough food for a few days. After she borrowed the cash she needed to buy two bus tickets, she took her two youngest children with her and caught the next Greyhound Bus going to Boston, Massachusetts. The older three children were left with my grandmother.

It was the middle of the winter in 1967. It had been snowing in Boston, and much snow was on the ground. Coming from Florida, we had no coats, and sandals were on our feet. My mother's cousin met us at the bus station. They had grown up together like sisters. Their mothers were sisters, and they lived together many years in the same house. My mother was an only child, and her cousin was the only girl in her family, so they were close. My mother said at that time she was a godsend. Our first stop was to Goodwill for hats, boots, and coats. Soon after, my mother got her own apartment. She worked, raised her children, and was at peace. The following year she sent for the rest of my siblings. Without her commitment to her children, only God knows where we would be.

In the summers, my mother would send me and my two sisters down to see my father and paternal grandmother. My father had gotten married and was doing well for himself and his family. My father had three daughters by my mother. Four years after I was born, my youngest sister became the new edition to the family. My father and his wife had no children together, but both had children from previous relationships. I knew that my father loved us. But as a child, I could never understand how he could take care of someone else's children and not care for his own. I still don't understand.

Children are the seeds that spring off from us. They are what is left after you are gone. Either they will sing your praises or nail your coffin shut. If we choose not to care for the seed, how could we ever expect a healthy harvest? The absence of a parent causes unnecessary discord. We can't keep waiting until our children are suicidal, violent toward others, or strung out on drugs before we are concerned. We must begin to ask, "What is wrong?" at the first signs of change. Not wanting to deal with your child's issues because you have so many of your own is neglect, and you don't have that right. When we become aware of our choices and understand that they affect everything around us, especially our children, our decisions will be altered. Children *do* have a lot of spring. But when that spring breaks, they are a to be reckoned with. And what they don't get as children, they will seek when they become an adult.

Children always have a way of blaming themselves when the parents are estranged. I also blamed myself for my father having very little to do with us. I always thought that if I would be better, he would love and care for us. I even thought that if I accomplished great things, then he would acknowledge that he loved me. Not just with words, but with actions. I spent a great deal of time trying to get his attention and approval. It never came. It took well into my adulthood to finally be okay with myself. I stopped looking for the validation I thought I needed. I now understand that God alone is all the approval that I need to be truly okay.

As a child with many insufficiencies—low self-esteem, lacking vision and direction in life, not knowing what real love was—I became a woman not knowing what it was to be loved by a man. I'm not talking about love that's temporary; that's lust. I'm not talking about emotional relationship love. This has become the way that most of us express our need for affection. I think we need to talk about it and stop acting like every person we spend a little intimate time with we attach the word *love* to. These are the loves that the world knows. And it may be the only love you know right now. That can change.

I'm talking love without conditions. Love that is not selfish or judgmental. Love that does not intentionally hurt. Love that does not enable. *Real* love is not jealous or insecure. The love I speak of is pure and can only be experienced through godly love from within. It is not triggered by what you do or say. It just is. Most of us will not admit that we have not experienced that kind of love. I am here to tell you that it is real, and you can experience it after you have done some house cleaning. I am referring to the house (body) that you live in. Once you move out the clutter, chaos, and disorder from within, what was there from the start will be revealed and accessible. It has taken many years for me to come to this realization. It's not because I am so smart. It took the love of God to come in and show me. I had been in many relationships: married, divorced, and children. I am still waiting for the day to experience true love between a man and a woman. It is the love that was always meant to be.

My mother had a house full of girls and chose to keep her personal life personal. She did not want to take the risk of exposing her girls to the perversion of possible abusers. My impression of healthy, intimate relationships was formed through insufficient evidence. It was through that distorted view that I would find the future of my unstable foundation.

During our summer vacation time, we would stay with my grandmother. My mother was concerned that we would not get treated well if we stayed with my father and his wife. Little did she know it would be my grandmother who would inflict the discontentment that rested in her upon me.

Truly, there is a fine line between love and hate. With much luck, few will find themselves living on the side of love. Many of us find ourselves somewhere in between the two. But there are those who find themselves on the side of hate too frequently. You see, I inherited my genetic features from my grandfather. I looked a lot like my grandfather whom my grandmother gravely hated. And with that, she highly disliked me as well. Every opportunity she got she displayed her disappointment in my presence. Aside from the name-calling, she would physically do things to me just to be cruel. She never did it in the presence of other adults. She wanted no evidence of her abusive behavior to ever be exposed, leaving me with only one conclusion to her madness; she knew exactly what she was doing. Her home was no safe haven for me. It was a place of dread and physical/emotional abuse.

The words spoken to a child help to shape his or her identity. Words are *not* just words. Words hurt! Words create! They write on the very soul of the recipient. Negative words are intended to hurt and to tear down one's self-esteem. These words also have an impact on the bystanders who hear them. These words and deeds influence the definition of what an adult is and what they are supposed to look like in character and personality. Corruption begets corruption.

Hands of the Deceiver

What do you do when no help is at hand? You give in. Being the quiet, meek, and timid little girl that life had already broken, it was all I knew. It was at the innocent age of five that I was sexually abused.

There was a family that lived downstairs in the basement apartment of our building. The family consisted of a mom and two children (boy and girl). The little girl was approximately seven years old. She had a teenage brother. It was through this relationship that this abuse began. I was extremely shy and quiet, and I had very few friends.

At the time, I had four older sisters. I was not surprised when they didn't invite me to play with them. I was truly a thorn in their side. I can count on one hand the amount of friends I had. Whenever I would go downstairs to play with this little girl, her older brother would always convince us to play house. This is where the deception began. Through these acts, he began a deceptive plan that would be progressively challenging for me. Playing on my innocence of youth, he began touching me inappropriately. With each "play" session, something new was added on. I always had to be the mother, and his sister would be our baby. He would explain, as he fondled me, this is what mommies and daddies do. I didn't know any different. I was only five and had not had the opportunity to see or even experience the act of healthy relationships. I did not have a clear understanding about personal boundaries and safe touching. I was also sworn to secrecy, and with threats of exposure, I was quickly entrapped in his web of deceit. I now believe that he was also abusing his little sister as well. Her trade off to her own safety was to allow it to happen to someone else. He would send her upstairs to get me to come out and play. Then, he would send her in the house and tell her to stay there in the bedroom until "Mommy or Daddy" comes to get her.

As time went on, my mother became suspicious. I was no longer allowed in anyone's house, so we played in the hallway. That's when the abuse increased. Ultimately touching turned to sodomy. I don't know exactly when. I just know that it did. My mother had to face that her baby—whom she had vowed to protect—was now being sexually assaulted. She did not know who it was. (I believe that after every traumatic act, I blocked out most of it.) My mother not only questioned me, but she interrogated me about the bloody undergarments I was wearing.

At five, I did not have the vocabulary to explain what was happening. She would accuse me of playing with the boys. I would keep proclaiming that I was not playing with any boys; I was just playing with my friend. In my mind, that was the truth. My mother would keep screaming at me, "Where did the blood come from!" I would answer, "I had to poop." I did not understand, and neither did she. It was not the typical assault that would happen to little girls who are raped. After each violation, I would be interrogated, accused, and beat. Punishment became the answer to my victimization. My mother was not equipped to handle what was happening. The thought of what was happening was so unbearable that she gave the responsibility of cleaning me up to my older sister. This act not only stole my innocence, but it damaged my family's mental and emotional wellness.

So I ask the question, what do you do when you don't know what to do? You do what you know. My mother was sexually abused as a child. When she told her mother, she was strongly reprimanded. Her mother did not know how to handle it because *she* was raped at twelve years of age. Being a virgin at the time, she did not understand this traumatic act of aggression. That rape produced a child by age thirteen. That child was my mother. My grandmother was a petite young girl. Giving birth at such a young age destroyed her inside, physically and emotionally. She was never able to bear children again. She had always wanted a house full of children, but her dreams of that would never come to fruition. My grandmother was then forced to marry her rapist in order not to bring shame upon herself and her family by having a child out of wedlock. With her father being a well-known gospel preacher, it caused them to make a decision that would distort her view of healthy relationships and a healthy self-image.

My mother thought that if she punished me hard enough, it would cause me to, "stay away from the boys." At five, I never saw myself as being around boys. I was just a little girl who wanted to play. So, I always denied being with them. That was my mind's truth. I was not trying to be deceitful. That's what I knew. Who would have thought that just wanting to play would cause so much trouble? This little girl didn't.

As time went on, somehow I kept finding myself being cornered by my perpetrator, followed by the assault, an interrogation, and another beating. Finally, my mother figured out most of what was happening. She confronted the family and threatened to kill them all if her daughter was ever touched again (that was my mom's personality). Without a doubt, they knew she was serious. That family moved that same week and was never heard from again. But the damage was already done.

Because of the abuse and victimization from the one person I thought I could trust, I lost my voice and became silent. Soon, my memory of the violence that I suffered diminished and eventually disappeared. The only trace of the offense was the memory of the bloody underwear and the beatings. It would take many years for me to regain the awareness of those horrible acts. That little girl of the past should have died. But she didn't. She is alive, safe, and still kicking.

As time went on, I complained very little. I learned that it was not safe to tell—and trust no one. It was safe to conclude that people will fail you even when they mean well. It may have not been a healthy approach, but it was all I had in order to survive.

CHAPTER 3

Change Don't Come Easy

When we know better, we do better. Until then, we continue on the road to insanity. The road to insanity is doing the same thing and expecting different results. In doing so, we find ourselves willing to settle for what it is we think we want and deserve. Life has a way of causing us to bow down to a lifestyle that was never intended for us.

No person can determine your ultimate destiny. Unless you have given them the power to do so, the choices still remain yours. If you have a checkered past, use it to become more diverse in your compassion for others. Life may have offered you lemons, but remember, lemonade can be a refreshing drink on a hot day. You may have even been abandoned, rejected, or abused. These things can cause you to be isolated in your troubles. What I have found out is that sometimes the less people I have around, the more I find myself talking to and hearing from God. This is a plus! Keep in mind that I am not talking about depression. That's a whole other issue! If you suffer from depression and you cannot get a grip on it, go see a specialist and get help.

You see, there are no tears left to this story. My ashes have been exchanged for the beauty of my Lord God. I am victorious and no longer a victim. He did not save me from my hurt, but He did erase the pain as if it had never happened. "Fear not, neither be thou confounded; for thou shall not be put to shame; for thou shall forget the shame of thy youth, and shall not remember the reproach of thy widowhood any more" (Isaiah 54:4). I share this scripture with you because in my midnight hour, God gave me this and I have held on to it ever since. It has been my strength. Remember that. It is not how you started the race that determines the winner; it is how you finish. You can finish this race and you can finish big.

Through the unveiling of life, I have found out that I can accomplish anything I want to. If I can see it, I can have it. A vision is essential for a successful future. As I mentioned earlier, your destiny must be God-led and not self-led. I cannot stress that enough. If you have not received a vision from God for your life, don't stop moving forward. Pray as you are moving and ask God to order your footsteps. Until you are clear on the direction you should walk in, don't change course. God knows how to find you right where you are. If you decide to stand still, you take the risk of becoming a paralytic. This does not include self-abuse or abuse at the hands of others. This is never okay. If you are dealing with issues of abuse in any form, seek help immediately. This behavior is an open door for fear.

Fear has a way of creeping into our thoughts and taking over. It will build a stronghold in your mind that will cause you to freeze in the middle of a busy highway (the highway of life). God has a plan for your life that is so much greater than you could ever imagine. We can, and do, sabotage our own future when fear steps in. Like I said before, when we don't know what to do, we do what we know. We know what is familiar. The familiar will cause your life to stand still (going backward puts your life at a standstill). In all honesty, these things did not work for us in the past, and it won't work now. Why would we think that it would work now? It could be that we are in a comfort zone. But comfort can be deadly.

Fear is a real feeling, but it is of the enemy. Fear is a seed planted for your destruction. We must push past fear to come to a new place. Yes, a new place is unfamiliar. The unfamiliar is necessary! In order to grow, you have got to go there. As my pastor always says, in order to get to where you are going, you have to be willing to leave from where you are at. We must move forward even while being afraid. It's the only way to get to the other side. When you get there, you will become upset with the enemy that held up your process. He is standing in the way of you receiving what is rightfully yours. You will then know that it took you way too long to possess your reward. Put fear aside and press on.

We could be in the way of our own progress. Sometimes we are waiting in what I call the halls of despair. These halls are lined with pictures of our past hurts, pains, and failures. We are so captivated with the angle that the photographer caught us at, or maybe we are entranced by the preciseness of the lighting in our moment of misery. So then we get comfortable and take a seat on the couch in this hallway. We kick off our shoes and enjoy a cup of coffee as we closely examine every displeasure that had snared us. Meanwhile, life goes on.

The journey isn't as difficult as we think. It is our perception of our situations that determines the longevity of our stay. We have been programmed to believe that in order to succeed or accomplish our hearts' desire, we need the support and affirmations of friends and family. When we put things in proper perspective, by taking responsibility for where we are, things look different. Then we become mindful of our decision-making process. We set ourselves up for good things to come our way. If you have trust in God, all you really need is His favor. The favor of God will open doors that no man can shut and close doors that no man can open. It is more valuable than money. It will take you before men and women of honor that you are not qualified to stand before. If you are in the hallway of despair, don't go down memory lane; look for the closest exit out of there. The journey continues on the other side of the exit door.

Tarnish Turns to Travail

What we go through doesn't have to stick to us. In most of our realities, it usually does. That was the case with me. After the sexual abuse had taken place, life went on as if nothing had ever happened. It was never talked about with me or even in my house.

Many years following the abuse, I continually found myself in situations with males who would try to convince me to have intercourse with them. I often experienced this at the hands of trusted family friends. I was forced to deal with their uninvited lustful weaknesses. By no means was I interested in their sexual gestures. I actually had a great fear in moving forward in anything that implied sexual contact. The impact of the physical abuse that followed the sexual abuse taught me to fear these implications. In my thoughts as a child, I knew it would cost me more pain. I was ashamed and embarrassed for them and for me. So I chose silence to be the weapon that I used against myself.

By the time I was twelve, I was overwhelmed with people taking advantage of me and taking me for granted. I remember going through a very quick transition. I can't explain what happened. It seems like I woke up one day and I was another person. Maybe I was. At that time, I had no memory of the past abuse. Still, the stained underwear never left me. It would periodically play in my head like a scene in a movie. It was like the abuse happened to someone else. The beatings that took place after the sexual abuse changed me forever. I continued into my teenage years with a new perspective. A large part of the shy, quiet, timid little girl was gone. She was hidden in the core of a developing teenager who was trying to figure out who she was and where she fit in society.

I did what I needed to do in order to fit in so that I would no longer be a target of other people's affection. Or so I thought. When innocence is taken from a child at such a young age, doors are opened to the enemy. They are defenseless and subjected to various trials. Abuse is an adult issue that was never intended for children to suffer. In it all, they must learn to travail past the mess that was never theirs to start with.

I found comfort in slowly being accepted by my sisters. They were quite verbal and tolerated very little in being taken sexually advantage of by men. They taught me how to get what I wanted without having to give up the goods. That's good, right? What they did not teach me was the consequences to selling out my soul. You might think, *What do you mean? You got what you wanted, and it didn't cost you anything.* If this is what you think, then you would be wrong. It cost me everything! My self-esteem, self-respect, respect for others, and ultimately my integrity left when I compromised "me."

I may have been broken, but the core of my creation had not changed. Let me say it another way. My original destiny that I was created to walk in had not changed. I chose to step off the path that was designed for me. I tried to fit into someone else's shoes. Stepping into someone else's shoes will cause you unnecessary pain. You can step into them, but when you begin to walk, you will suffer from bunions, blisters, corns, and callouses. Their shoes will rub you in places you did not know shoes could even touch. Wherever the point of contact, you will suffer. It will deliver great pain to your whole body. Those who think that they are smart and can get around this will put pads into the shoes. Sometime tissue may even work for a while. Eventually, you will have to take those shoes off.

Take some time to soak your tired, aching feet. Scrub those corns and callouses off, and get you a new pair of shoes that fit. The pain is a symptom of notice. You have stepped into the wrong pair of shoes. Some shoes can be too big. Life will then rub you in ways that cause surface injury. If they are too small, the shoe seams will eventually bust, and your whole foot will be exposed. Over a long period, wearing the wrong shoes will cause deformation of your feet, and you may walk with a limp. This will slow you down, and the world will know you are injured.

We all have a purpose. In that purpose, there are people assigned to us for us to give comfort, direction, and wisdom to. It is for us to do our part, not assign it to someone else. If we are not in the right place, we miss that opportunity that is allotted to us to bring change into this world. If they meet up with the wrong person, the results could be lasting and devastating.

Each one of us has a responsibility for lost souls—the Great Commission. We are accountable for the road we have led them on and left them on. Whether it is of good or evil, we will account for them. It is never too late to get back on track and guard your post from intruders. You will be rewarded for your work in the end. Serve with all you know and leave the rest up to God. He is able to fill in the gaps.

In seeking to find my place in society, I gave all that I had left—my body. At the age of seventeen, I had my first child. I broke my mother's heart. The plans she had for me were not what I could live up to. My father exclaimed that he always knew I was not going to be anything, saying that all I was going to do was have a house full of babies. When he would say, "You're just like your mother," I suppose he was referring to my children as well. I have four beautiful sons that God has blessed me with. It has been a long road in raising them. I am a single mother. For the majority of my children's lives, I raised them alone. Hands down, it is the hardest job I have ever had to do. For those of you who have one, thank God for him/her. If you have two, it is good for the household. They can keep each other company. If you have three or more, God be with you. Especially, if they are close in age. This is insanity on another level. I believe there are rewards in it, and I am still waiting. Somebody owes me something! (Smile) Before anyone gets mad, I'm just kidding.

In the midst of a lot of serious, overwhelming issues, you have got to learn how to laugh or you will eventually crack just like a clay vessel. Ask me how I know! My brokenness did not lead to me being hospitalized, but I came pretty darn close. Luckily, I had friends and family around me that came to my rescue. Weeping on the floor in a corner of a room balled up like a frightened little girl asking where my deceased mother was and why did she leave me like this was close enough to "losing it" for me. I was in my right mind, but I was standing on the edge of a cliff willing to jump off and knowing that I would not be willing to come back. It was one of the most frightening things I had ever experienced. I wanted and needed relief from all of life's pressures. I wanted to take that step off the cliff, but I kept thinking, *My children will have no one to take care of them.* I even got to the point that when I would nap during the day, I would say to God, "It's okay if You take me now; I am in a good place with You. I am ready to go." I would close my eyes and sleep. Shortly after, I would awake again. I was still here with the same issues, but just enough strength to make it through the day. I want you to understand that I was never suicidal. I was tired of travailing. It was my hope, if possible, for the world to stop spinning long enough for me to step off and breathe.

When things happen at inopportune times, they are what I call curve balls. These balls are pitched, and many of them tend to hit their targets. Life still proceeds with you or without you. This will leave you bruised but not broken. As life proceeds and you have many hidden issues from the past that have not been dealt with, this is a good combination for a train wreck. We won't even talk about two trains colliding in passing. We'll save that discussion for another book another day. A train wreck leaves very few survivors. Those who survive are so traumatized that their body chemistry can be altered and medication is necessary to bring the body back to a normal balance. Most train wrecks can be avoided. It does take some planning, effort, and eventually hard work. The work is on the issues that have not been dealt with.

Many years have passed and we are moving along as if all is well. If you know you have issues from the past that you have not dealt with, one curve ball can cause a devastating train wreck. This is strategically planned by the enemy—Satan. It is his job to set you up. You can be saved or unsaved; curve balls thrown for your destruction can and will cause severe damage and, in some cases, fatalities. Seek help for yourself *before* the wreck. It could save your life. When we choose to stay in denial and not get help, that's insanity on another level!

CHAPTER 4

Insanity on Another Level

Once I became a teenager, I hung with an older crowd. I had earned the right to hang out with my older sisters and their friends. I was old enough to do what they were doing. By thirteen, I was partying, drinking, and smoking cigarettes and marijuana. Over the next few years, this activity would progress to heavier drugs like cocaine and pills. I had never associated any of my past with my current behavior. I was just fitting in and having what I thought was fun.

I started dating my first son's father nineteen months prior to giving birth at the age of seventeen. I was not ready for a relationship, and my only reason for having intercourse was to get it over with. At the time, having sex at sixteen was considered pretty old. That is the danger with peer pressure. I was so tired of the peer pressure about having sex that I told one of my sisters and her boyfriend to find me somebody to sleep with. It may sound crazy, but I had no desire to seek out someone for myself. A couple of weeks later, they had chosen my sister's boyfriend's best friend. I just said "whatever" and started talking to him. Shortly after that, I had sex with him "just because." I didn't enjoy it at all. I had no real interest or attraction to him, but he was nice. So, I did it! Insanity on another level? Yeah. Whatever!

We dated for five years all together. The last two years of the relationship had turned violent. At the time, I did not identify it as domestic violence. He was 6'3" and weighed about 285 pounds. Somehow I though the fight was fair with me at 5'9" and 150 pounds. Obviously, fighting back was not that effective. The insanity is that I was going back and forth to court during all the violent episodes, and making out the incident reports. Shortly afterward, I would get right back with him, and we would go to the courthouse together. I never dropped any charges. I told the truth every time about what took place. I would tell him that he had no right putting his hands on me and if they locked him up and give him time, it would be fine with me. I wanted to make sure that if something happened to me, like death, that I would have a running record of the abuse I was tolerating. Insanity? Yes! Insanity on another level.

I finally left him after I had enough. I knew that nothing was going to change unless I made the change. At the age of twenty-one, I thought that making a change meant finding another partner who would treat me better. You may be thinking, *What's wrong with that?* The problem is that "you" will take "you" with "you" wherever "you" go. I had every right to leave, but I didn't have the right to bring somebody else into my mess, and that's what I did.

About a month after leaving my son's father, I met a really nice guy (we are still friends until this day). We started dating and everything I was going through fell on him. He found himself having to watch his back everywhere he went just as I did. He continually had physical altercations with someone he did not know because of who he chose to be with. His home that he shared with his sister was being vandalized. Many other things happened that caused great distress for him and his family. This was not his problem originally. I needed an out, and he was it. It

$5 FAVORITES

3 DAYS ONLY

POPEYES®

2 PCS MIXED CHICKEN*
or 3 TENDERS
or POPCORN SHRIMP
&
2 REG SIDES • 1 BISCUIT

Valid 11/21/16 - 11/23/16

$5
PLUS TAX

POPEYES

CORP-EOM-11

was a great price to pay to be with someone you would not spend the rest of your life with.

It is not okay for you or me to put our issues on someone else. We call it love, or something of the sort. When it's all said and done, they walk away messed up because of our mess. Then, the pattern of abuse continues. People are not born messed up. You don't wake up with a bad attitude and continue in that for the rest of your life. People don't come into this world mean, mad, withdrawn, and hateful. Life changes people. What I put on him would take years for him to take off. Listen ladies, you know we get together and have these talks about how wonderful he is, and we throw in all the issues of "the only thing is . . ." And then we say, "I really love him though." Keep in mind that his issues usually come from someone like you and me. We have learned to love wrong because we have not loved ourselves first. That's why some people accept so much mistreatment in a relationship.

So, let's get real. As much as men mess women up, we mess them up as well. If we both took the time to be emptied out before the next "date," we would be healthier as a nation. Real people continually strive to get better. They know they are not perfect. It is a lot of work to be your best. It starts with honesty. It is not easy looking at your flaws and calling them what they are. Stop acting like you don't care. That's an issue within itself! Stop acting like you just want to get your groove on. Stop acting like you don't want or need anybody. Only God can help you out of this. You must acknowledge you need His help. If you could do it on your own, you would have by now.

My deepest desire is for you to have peace, happiness, joy, true love, and a new value for life. None of this is possible without healing. If I have painted myself as some angel, forgive me. These traumatic experiences were real and they changed me. Yes, life happens, but I had choices and I made many wrong choices for myself. I eventually chose not to let this be my handicap and I surrendered!

In my teenage years, I became a liar, cheater, thief, user, adulterer, manipulator, verbally cussed out men, and much more. With all of that, I still could not understand how the world could not see the real me. I did not even know the real me. The problem was that I saw the nice stuff, but I could not relate to the other stuff. I even denied that any of this stuff belonged to me. Yep, you're right, insanity!

My problem was that I never identified what and whom my problem was with. It was with me! I did not realize that running to another relationship would only compound the issues. I am not here to judge you by any means. I am no better than you are. Healed, but not better. There is one letter between "your" and "our" and that is "Y" or "why." Sometimes we can be judgmental in trying to understand someone else's situation. If we do a real self-check first, we will have greater compassion for them. So, let's not ask the why "he" or "she" and begin to ask why "I"? We are so closely joined together in life that we forget our sisters and brothers are not that different than we are. Life can cause us to slip and fall. So the next time you see someone down, lend a hand to pull him or her up. The next target of the enemy could be you.

CHAPTER 5

Pushed Past Patience

After I had broken up with my son's father, I remember him saying that if he could not have me, then no one else would. I did not take it that seriously until he started walking it out. Every day I received threatening phone calls. He stalked me and paid others to do the same. They would give him the rundown of my whereabouts. Only hours after I would change my phone number, he would be calling with the harassment all over again. I believe he would pay people who worked at the telephone company to get my telephone number. After changing my number several times, I realized that I was wasting money. I felt alone and thought there was no way out of this. I was pushed past patience.

The emotional abuse really started to get to me. Apparently, he had a set of keys to my house, which I was unaware of. One day, he came into my house when I was not home and destroyed all the clothes I owned. He took my jewelry, underwear, and lingerie. Later I found out he had given these items to his current girlfriend. He took pictures that I had of myself, ripped the heads off them, and wrote threatening notes on them. This was the craziness that I pulled someone else into.

Numerous times, I would be sitting in someone else's house, and a brick would come flying through the window. He wanted to intimidate others so that they would not want me to be at their home. It was ugly!

I finally had enough. I was pushed to a place that no one wants to go. I had decided that I was not going to deal with it anymore. I was not safe and no one could do anything to help me. Something had to be done. I needed to take control. I had sought out support from family and friends. He had already been manipulating them through this process. The things he was doing to me he told everyone that I was doing them to him. There was so much confusion that no one wanted to get involved. Not even my mother.

Alone and isolated, I decided that we both could not live on this earth. I settled within myself that if I did not kill him, he was going to kill me. I borrowed a gun from someone I knew. He showed me how to use it, and I was all set. That day I sat in my house prepared. That evening the threatening calls came in as usual. This time, I responded differently. I told him to come on by. I let him know I was alone and waiting for him. I sat and waited with my door unlocked. To my surprise, that night he did not show up.

I thank God he didn't. He would have died that day, and I would have been spending the rest of my life in prison for murder. I cannot say this enough: when God has purpose in you, rest assured, it will come out. He will not go against your will, but if you give it over to Him, He will see you through. Everything I have been through can be used to help someone else. It's all for the glory of God.

The court system is much kinder today than it was years ago. Back then, in order to arrest an abuser, they had to catch the person in the act or at the scene violating a restraining order. It didn't make much sense. Who stops in the middle of a beating to allow you to call the cops on them?

Domestic violence is a very serious issue. For those who have not suffered the abuse, it is difficult for them to understand why someone would stay in a harmful situation. This type of violence is more mental than physical. It is meant to depower the individual. It is one of the greatest forms of control. It deals with the psyche of the victim. You are a victim and will remain to be until you take your power back. By doing something about it, you are victorious in every sense of the word. Although things can sometimes get worse before they get better, the fact that you stood up is worth applauding. When you have been broken down mentally, physically, and emotionally, the burden of leaving and having a hope for tomorrow becomes almost unthinkable.

Many women lost their fight due to the injustice of the judicial system. Even more importantly, they lost their life. Never forget that someone else has paid the price for us so that we may have the resources that are available today. I thank God for the revision of the laws. It is only by the grace of God that I am still here. We have the right to live in peace and have freedom from all abuse. You deserve better if you are in an abusive situation. Take care of yourself and those around you. You are worth it!

There was another incident that took place after I broke up with my son's father. He had come to the house to pick up my son for his visit. At the time, I was talking to a male friend (truly a friend) who had stopped by for a brief visit. To my surprise, my son's father rushed into the house and without a word he grabbed the guy, hung him out of the third-floor window, and threatened to drop him. He then turned on me and beat me almost to a pulp. That was a beating that got me another ride in the ambulance. When I went to court for these charges, the judge told me that the next time he comes to pick up his son, that I was to make sure I don't have company. He was the sitting judge for all of the domestic violence cases that came through that court at that time. There was no one else to bring my case before. I remember feeling violated by my abuser and the system.

Sometimes the justice system renders no justice at all. I stayed in court continually. The only thing that was said to him was, "The next time we will lock you up." My thought was, *The next time! Hello! What about this time, and is there going to be a next time for me?* That judge was removed from his position the following year due to the death of an abused victim who could not get results from her restraining order in his court.

The police knew me so well that I had a direct number to the domestic violence unit that was established in the police department. I had an officer I was assigned to. She would keep track of my court case and handle all of my domestic issues and calls after the fact. They really encouraged me to go into hiding. They knew I was at great risk for losing my life, but I refused to hide. I felt like I did not want to give him that much power over my life. The police would frequently patrol my street and surrounding areas. They kept watch out for him on every shift. But there was only so much they could do. As well meaning as some people and things may be, sometimes it's still not enough.

The pain that I suffered is validated when it can bring awareness and healing to others. Am I my sister's keeper? Yes, I am. I had to come through all of this to show you there is hope and completeness on the other side. The question is, are you willing to cross over that river? I will not lie to you. There probably won't be a bridge to carry you over. You will have to get in the water and learn to swim. You will get wet and the water may be cold, but you will not drown and you will make it over. I did, and I believe you will also.

A year later, my first son's father was killed in a car accident. I remember receiving the news. It was surreal. I had no thoughts or feelings about it. I was numb. A few hours later, it all hit me at once. I found myself quickly falling into a deep depression. I could not cry. I was sad for my son. I was sad for myself. I had wanted to see him suffer the same way he made me suffer. Then I thought, *How dare he die and leave me with all of this responsibility to raise my son alone.* I was mad at God and angry at him. I felt like God should have taken me instead and left him here to deal with all of this stuff. I had already suffered enough. How dare he die and get away without suffering for all that he did to me. I know this sounds like insanity on another level. It's not! Trauma on overload can cause you to say things that sound quite rational to you in that moment. But to someone else, it's completely irrational. I probably sounded suicidal, but I really wasn't.

I have recognized that when God has a plan for your life, God will move heaven and earth to bring about His purpose in your life. It may sound quite repetitious, but it's real. I remember saying to my mother, "Why didn't God take me instead?" That is not the question to ask a mother. But she answered it as a strong woman and a friend. She said, "Maybe God left the best person to raise your son." Unfortunately, a few weeks later, a drug dealer supplied me with all the cocaine and champagne I could handle, in celebration of my graduation as a computer repair tech. I was high for the next three weeks, and I went from a size 12 to a size 8. I decided then that anything that would do this to me in such a short period of time was not anything I needed. I realized I had not properly dealt with my son's father's death. Thank God for mercy.

The enemy knows the distractions to send your way. I was very vulnerable at that time and it did not take much to get a yes out of me. Once again, my manipulation skills were at use. I knew that he was hoping to get something from me, and I used that to get all that I wanted without it costing me a dime. That was the mindset I lived in. It's the mode of a survivor. There were many risks that I took with the use of drugs and alcohol and such things. By the grace of God, I never became an addict. He kept me in ways I still don't understand. God had a plan for my life and He knew that if He had let me go, He would have lost me forever.

It took many, many, years before I understood that it was not my will power that got me through things, but it was God protecting what He had put in me. As messed up as I was, I still had a destiny to be fulfilled. And I had a merciful God Who still wanted to complete what He had started.

I encourage you to travail through the pain. The process may be long and tedious, but hang in there. You have come too far to give up now. God is with you on this path, and I am too. With God, you will never be alone. Your greatest value is your spirit. Your spirit is the only thing that is eternal. We invest a lot in our children, family, marriage, career, and material goods. In the end, the only thing that will last is the investment you have made into your spirit. I wish somebody would have told me these things years ago. Sometimes we hear without understanding. Seek understanding; it is life. Without it, there is no real growth.

A Method to My Madness

After the death of my son's father, I felt like I needed a change of pace. I moved back to Florida after twenty years. I found a beautiful condo-style apartment less than a mile from the Orlando Airport. This newly built development was known for its award-winning landscape designed with fountains. I was blessed. At the same time, I was scared.

Pretty much everyone who lived there was business owners, pilots, and stewardesses. After a few weeks, I had me a fabulous apartment. I moved in with the few items that I had and settled in for the ride. I learned to fit in, and I socialized very little in my new neighborhood. It was a little bit of heaven on earth. The only environment I had known was that of the inner city. This new culture was almost more than I could stand. I had walked into a blessing, but it was very difficult to live in it. I felt like a fish out of water.

I lived in Orlando for about a year and a half. I had the best time. I did my share of partying, drinking, and dating. I went to church faithfully and even went to the Wednesday-night Bible studies. One thing I can say about the people in the South is they believe in going to church. So after spending all Saturday night with my boyfriend, we'd get up and go to church. He went to his church and I went to mine. We'd kiss and say, "I'll see you later." I thought all was well, and no one told me any different.

Going to church and saying a nice prayer does not make you a Christian, neither does it make you saved. It's a start, but there is much more to it than that. You must have a change of heart. A transformation must happen on the inside, and then change will show up on the outside. I had no conviction about anything I was doing. I was comforted in knowing that I was doing what others in the church were doing. I played a very dangerous game with my natural and spiritual life. I was living life, having fun, and going to church. I was casually dating a few guys at the time. There was one who got very close to me. I made him a promise that I knew I could not keep. I had gotten caught in the midst of my own mess. The sad part of this whole story is that I really liked this one. He would have been my #1 choice to settle down with. The one thing that I will never forget is the pain and disappointment that was in his eyes the night he found out there were others. It pierced my soul.

It's fair to say that he lost all trust in me, and us, that night. Although we still remained friends over the years and continued a sexual relationship as well (until God pricked my heart), things were never the same. This experience changed him forever. I watched as he was no longer able to trust or commit in his future relationships.

This is what I mean when I say that we don't have that right to draw others into our mess. When I met him, I had convinced him to leave his baby momma because I thought she was doing him wrong. Then I came along and did the same thing!

I was always hoping I would have the opportunity to win him over again and to do it right. It never happened. It took many years for me to let this one leave my life and my heart. I knew I had to take full responsibility for all I had done, and I needed to ask God for forgiveness.

Before I left Boston and moved to Florida, I had met my future husband at a wedding. We hit it off and continued our communication while I was in Florida. He had moved down to Florida about a year later. Things did not work out for him in Florida. The South and the North clashed. So we both decided to move back to Boston. I knew that if we were going to have a fighting chance in our relationship, I had to leave Florida. After moving back to Boston, all was well for a while. I found an apartment and me, my son, and my now fiancé moved in together once again.

Sadly, it wasn't long before we broke up. I found myself seeking God for the first time with my whole heart. I found a new church home, and they embraced me in a way I had never experienced before. They were loving and attentive. They seemed genuinely concerned about me and my son's well-being. This loving "church" ended up being a cult. Feeling trapped and not knowing how to get free, I married my ex-fiancé. I thought he could help me get out of this cult. Instead, he joined in.

Thank God, it didn't take long for him to figure it out. He got out and that released me of my obligation to participate since my commitment was to my husband. It was a little more complicated than that. He actually called them out and all of that love they were showing me stopped. We were completely shunned from the church. I was trying to live right and commit to the things of God. So when all of this happened, it really threw me for a loop. I did lose faith and hope in the church. It would take twelve years for me to come back to my rightful place. Didn't I say in an earlier chapter that change don't come easy? Hell had grabbed me and took me for the ride of a lifetime. Once again, I went back to what I knew. I say no more.

By twenty-six, I found myself married and on my second son. I had settled into the married life pretty well. It was not all that I thought it would be, but I enjoyed the idea of being married. I was there for the long hall. Shortly after my son's first birthday, I experienced another life-changing event.

It was raining lightly and the roads were wet. I approached a stop light. I put my foot on the brake and the car hydroplaned and spun out of control. I have heard people use the phrase, "my life flashed before my eyes" when having a near-death experience. This time I understood it. God showed me that I was supposed to die in this car accident, but my child, who was in the back in a car seat, would live. I don't know how long I was spinning, but when the car came to a stop, the car's bumper was right up against a storefront. The driver's side door was almost pinned against a huge, steel light pole. I believe angels are real and in action. Although this was not enough to send me back to church, I knew there would be so much more to my story. I said, "God, You have something for me to do." I knew it with everything in me. I didn't really share that with people, but I hid this away in my heart with other things.

After a while, we began to have problems in our marriage. There was a lot of dysfunction in our relationship. Our communication consisted of swearing, name calling, and finger pointing. Take note of this: when you choose to be with someone who has issues, you probably have greater ones. Do not settle for this. It is toxic and you will become toxic too. You may not want to hear this, but it's true. The environment is toxic and it affects everyone in it, even the children. This is disrespectful, degrading, and establishes insecurity and inferiority complexes in your partner. It eats away at the soul and the spirit of a person. I don't disagree to the fact that it probably was there before you met them, but it doesn't make it right for you to become the perpetrator that continues the abuse is what I am saying. Marriage should be about love and respect for one another. Please do not justify this behavior by saying to yourself he or she does it to me; therefore, I do it in return. Then, I would have to ask why do you allow this? It's not love. It's something else. I can attest to where I have been in my own life and the results of others. This behavior is destructive and should be unacceptable.

We decided to go to marriage counseling. In the midst of it all, we separated. Not legally, just mutually. I remember we had an on-fire dispute. He said one of the cruelest things that a man can say to his wife. He said, "I am no longer attracted to you. You don't turn me on and that's why I go to strip clubs to get turned on by someone else." If there is a man out there reading this book, please never say that, even if you feel that way. There is another way to express your displeasure. It felt like he had just chewed me up and spit me out into the trash. I said to him after I calmed down some, "We need to think about if this marriage is what we both want." I told him that over the next few months we both needed to prepare for a separation if that was what we decided to do. Both of us had some form of income coming in, but neither one of us had stored up for a rainy day.

After sitting in silence for about five minutes, he got up, packed his clothes, and headed for the door. He turned and said to me, "I will be at my father's house if you need me." I remember sitting there thinking, *What just happened? My husband walked out on me and the children with no more discussion than that.* I should have been asking him how he knew that he could go to his father's house unless he had already been planning this. I was so overwhelmed I could not think straight.

The following day we talked. He said, "I left because you put me out." I was totally confused. Instead of arguing the point, I said nothing more about that but argued about a lot of other things. I thought in time this would blow over. It really never did. By this time, my self-esteem was under the doormat. I took on the responsibility that it was my fault he was gone. He had to have been right. I put him out, right? I decided that my marriage failed because of me. The children did not have a father. I had not been a good mother, wife, friend, or lover, and anything else you could think of. I did it all with a smile. I would not want to leave out the fact that I was a full-time student, I had a toddler and a ten-year-old to care for alone, and it was two weeks before Christmas.

My husband paid $50 a week for child support for his son only. Since my oldest son's father had passed when he was four years old, my husband was the only father he knew. It was like a knife stabbing me in the heart to know that my decisions were negatively affecting him. This rejection was coming fast and hard, and I had caused it all. Little drops of poison with every distorted perception. I accepted whatever he said because, after all, it was my fault.

My husband and I continued to be intimate. He came by once a week to pay his wife her due. You know what I mean? It was really to make sure that I was not sleeping with anyone else. I knew within myself that he was not being faithful. I just could not bring myself to the place of saying no to him at that time. Even until this day, I never told him the impact that his decision had on me. (There did come a time that I had to face things as they really were and release myself from accountabilities that were never mine.) I punished myself secretly for many years. All of that self-affliction showed up in my actions and my mental and emotional state. Trust me; I did hit rock bottom. Months later, I filed for a legal separation. I had asked him several times if he still wanted the marriage, and he always responded with, "I'm not sure." I knew it was a nice way of saying no, yet still keep his foot in the door of my life. I finally went to court and moved on to the next relationship.

The guy I met was really nice, he treated me like a queen, and he loved my kids. The problem was that I was still emotionally stuck in my marriage. Once my husband found out that I was dating someone else, it was his new mission to get his wife back. After about a year, he did. It was not long before he dropped a bomb in my lap. He had gotten someone pregnant. I was crushed! Sick with anger, I pressured him into making her get an abortion. Little did I know I would not be able to let it go. We muddled through another year together before we separated again.

I moved on to the next relationship. Yes, things were quickly spinning out of control (with a smile still on my face). This time, I met my match. I fell for this new guy kind of hard. He was smooth talking, cunning, and a laid-back gentleman. He was right up my alley. Six months into the relationship, he cheated on me. I was crushed. Even my marriage didn't do this to me. I think it's because it came from out of nowhere. I was floored. I had never had anyone to cheat on me and then deny he was dating me right to my face. There really was a method to my madness. Believe it or not, this was the beginning of my transformation process. It would take many years to unravel all of the stuff from my past to become the new creature I am today.

CHAPTER 6

Really, Who Are You?

Please try not to get caught up in my past drama. If you do, you will be stuck there by yourself. I am not there anymore, and I have moved on. I share in detail because I know that I am not alone in my story. If you are still stuck in the past, I am here to tell you there is hope for freedom. If God did it for me, I know He will do it for you.

I walked into a new year full of hope. It was short lived by a web of deception that was being spun for me and by me. Entangled in trickery, I lost sight of who I was and where I was going. My web was tangled up with his web and someone else's. Have you ever seen ten different threads all meshed together? You don't know where one starts and another ends. There's no other word for a mess but a mess and that's what my life had become.

One Saturday evening I called my boyfriend, and a woman answered. She asked who was calling, and I told her, "His girlfriend." I heard a discussion going on in the background. When he got on the line, I lost it! I really let him have it. If it wasn't so cold outside, I would have driven over there. If you understand New England weather in January, it was below zero with high winds. I did not lose it that much, and I certainly was not that crazy. There really was a limit to my madness and, at that point, it was the cold.

The next day, after I had calmed down, I went over there to retrieve my things from his house. I was calm enough to have a rational conversation with both him and the other woman. Getting mad at her wouldn't have solved anything. I had to learn the hard way that if he truly loved me, he would have been with me, not her. We cleared the air, and I told her she could have him. Days later, I ended up sleeping with him. If that wasn't bad enough, I made it a point to let his new girlfriend know what happened. I wanted her to know that he did the same thing to her (cheated) as he did with me.

Listen ladies, why do we feel like we have to be all up in the other woman's face fighting over some man who did not honor us? If that's love, we can all do without it. If he was yours, he would have been yours and not hers. After a lie is exposed, who we *really* are shows up. Think about the last time you were faced with some drama. It doesn't have to be another woman. The real you showed up with jeans on and ready to take on what was next. I'm just saying, let's be honest. Most of the time, the other woman does not even know you exist. If he's your husband and she knows he's married, now you have a fight. He's the one you are in covenant with. He's the one who broke the vow between you, not her. I have been told that power not channeled into purpose equals death. The power I had was truly misdirected, and I was rapidly dying inside.

That day, something broke inside of me. I was angry and I felt so much hatred toward him. There was so much ugliness inside of him. I saw him as evil and monstrous. A friend of mine once said to me, "The person you are with is a reflection of who you are. They are your mirror image." I thought that idea was preposterous and I was offended. How dare she say that? I was not like him. No way! Over the course of that week, she kept proclaiming the same thing and I kept denying it. Then, it hit me like a ton of bricks. I *am* just like him! I am a liar, a cheat, a manipulator, self-focused, and don't care who I hurt in the process as long as I get what I want. I was doing it all under the radar. No one knew, not even me.

I wept in my brokenness. It was hard to believe the facts of who I was. In all reality, there was nothing he was doing to me that I had not done to him or someone else. And I hated him because I hated myself. Somewhere within me the truth had already shown up. I became mentally and emotionally burnt out. When you have to face yourself in the midst of hurting, it intensifies your experience. I felt like I was in a living hell!

In a truth-defining moment, only God can help you through it. You can choose to continue hiding, but the truth will never go away. It will haunt you. There will be no peace in you unless you begin to face those night visions in the light of day.

Finally, God had pulled the covers off my sins. I had to make a choice at that point. Would I continue the game of charades or would I choose something new? That new thing was change. I called out to God in tears and said, "Help me to change. I hate what I see. I don't want to be like this anymore." For weeks, it was hard for me to look in the mirror. Every time I did, I saw what I really was. I avoided the mirror as much as possible. In the mornings, I would shower and fix my face. I avoided any reflection of truth for the rest of the day. The one person I could not get away from appeared everywhere I went. That was me.

I felt so exposed, naked. It seemed like everyone knew everything I had ever done. I was embarrassed, ashamed, and hurting. I just wanted to be covered, but it was too late. For the first time, I understood how Adam and Eve felt in the Garden. After they sinned, their eyes were opened. When the scales fell off of my eyes, nothing was hidden anymore. I could scc everything so much clearer. Have you ever walked down the street butt naked? Well, me either. That's just the way it felt. I accepted the fact that I was not as good as I thought. I was nowhere near good at all. My perception of myself was way off. All of this helped to position me for my destiny.

It's funny how we sometimes view ourselves. Either we place ourselves on a pedestal to be above or we see ourselves as dirt on the ground. Neither of these is factual. We all fall somewhere in the middle. Change doesn't come easy, but if change is to come at all, you have to want it for yourself. No one can want it for you or make it happen. As hard as your process may be, trust me, it won't kill you.

I was still on speaking terms with my husband. I say *my husband* because at that time I was not divorced yet. I had been confiding in him about what I was going through. He was quite understanding and encouraged me to move on. He told me that I was too good for this guy anyway. In his consolations, he was getting what he wanted from me as well. I found myself sleeping with both of them because I never completely cut off the relationship that I was trying to get over. I was completely open with both of them about what was going on. They both chose to stay. After about a month of doing this, I received a letter that was slipped under my door. It was from the young lady who was previously involved with my husband. The note read that she was now pregnant again and she was due in a few months.

I had many cracks in my vessel. A new crack appeared with every incident of hurt, pain, abuse, or rejection. It felt like my vessel was on the verge of shattering. But God had a hold on me. I may have not known it at the time, but I am sure of it today.

Through all of this drama, the greatness that had been lying dormant in me began to emerge. A paradigm shift had taken place, and it started with me. Something woke up inside of me, and love poured out toward others. I went from being the woman who slept with other women's men to proclaiming to women that we must care for one another. The fight that was in me had worn me down so much that when God stepped up, I was open and available to Him. I was committed never to cheat, date, or entertain anyone else's mate. I knew that the pain I experienced was the pain that I caused for others, and that was never my intention. I am happy to say that I will continue to fulfill that commitment. I made a conscious decision to never do that again. This is ugly, painful, and disrespectful to everyone involved in this type of saga. There is a greater value on you than just your back! These acts are a reflection of what you really feel about yourself. Sometimes change is only one decision away. In this life, it is never just about us. Our actions affect others, and they are usually innocent in the matter.

I was not aware of the impact my past had on my present actions. You cannot change what you don't acknowledge. I had to begin to see me. Self-hate is a hard thing to change. The first step in walking the right path is asking for forgiveness—God's forgiveness and forgiveness from others. You must be willing to be transparent and turn from your offenses—repent.

Forgiveness is really for you, not the ones who offended you. If the mention of their name or the thought of what they have done to you sends you into an abyss of negative emotions (depression, anger, rage, etc.), they own you! Until you are free from that, you are in bondage to it, and they hold the key to your release. You have got to take the key from them and unlock the yoke that is upon your neck. The only one who can take the key from your perpetrator is you. Stand up and take control of yourself and your life. There comes a time when we have to reach above ourselves. True strength comes from above. When you invite God into your life, He will work with you to help you release the chains of bondage and become free. Being free is a God thing. God is the best gift that you can give to yourself. Forgiveness is not something you are capable of doing on your own. You may say the words, but it will take divine intervention to erase the offense from your soul. A great offense will not leave you easily. You will need help. Somewhere along the way, you will look up and say, "God, I need Your help." Then, you will recognize that it was Him all the long who was there with you pulling you through.

This is a little side bar. When you see someone spinning out of control, don't ask them about what's going on. It's deeper than that. Find out what has happened to cause them to disrespect themselves and others. Why would you use and punish your body as a weapon against yourself? You usually have some idea. I am here to tell you that it is always deeper than what you think. There is hurt, pain, fear, rejection, and more at the root of these actions. The problem is, no one wants to stay around long enough to help you dig through your trash containers. Not even the specialist. So, they write you a prescription and tell you to come back next Tuesday at the same time, until your insurance runs out. I'm not knocking doctors or drugs. I'm just telling you that it is not your final answer. Some people need drugs to stay balanced. Most people do not need it forever. There has to be a time when complete healing must take place if you are going to be free or have any real peace sustained in your life. I say this because I have been there too (counseling, therapy). It was an opportunity to help me talk things through and come up with my own answers. I just needed to calm down, and you may need to do the same.

There is a process by which complete healing comes forth and emotional clarity is developed. It is called developed pain. Developed pain is healthy and requires continuous maintenance to stay pure. It is a place where the past can no longer impact the present or future. It does not need affirmation from others because it has been empowered through development. It takes responsibility and control for future outcomes in life. Developed pain understands that sometimes things will get worse before it gets better. It understands that what is, is not what used to be. It may look the same, but it's not the same. Developed pain celebrates where it has been and where it is going to. It understands that its perception of situations and circumstances makes the difference in the mental outcome of where it stands today and tomorrow. Developed pain is healed, delivered, and released.

Undeveloped pain is different. This pain is a place of emotional despair. It breeds bitterness, anger, condemnation, evil thoughts, and intentions. It leaves its victims powerless and under the control of people who are probably no longer in its sphere. Over time, it transforms a loving, kindhearted person into a venom-spewing serpent waiting to attack. It preys on negativity and self-condemnation. It doesn't possess the character to ever build up; it only tears down. It lacks self-confidence and avoids any form of trust. It desires to trust, but cannot deliver. It seeks negative attention and thrives on self-pity. Even when its intentions are at their best, it breeds corruption. It extracts life out of the best of us if we are not guarded. This pain comes to steal, kill, and destroy all hope, dreams, and destinies. Do not give your time to it; it reeks of death.

In this life, it is important to complete this process of healing. If you don't, you will never know who you really are. You will begin to look at others to find out who you are. In doing so, you mimic what you see. And the identity of who you are gets lost in the fantasy of your imagination. If you like the way someone walks, you'll adopt her stride. If you like the way Mary laughs and throws her hair to the side, you will do that too. You may even resort to liposuction, a tummy tuck, or plastic surgery on your eyes, lips, and nose to look like someone else. Pretty soon, you are no longer you. Congratulations! The problem is, you are now the Bride of Frankenstein. You have lost your identity, and you don't even know it.

And through it all, you smiled! In the quiet, midnight hours you no longer laugh. There is loneliness and overwhelming sadness, and you wonder what is wrong with you. Remember, your uniqueness is a gift from God. He is the only One Who truly knows you. He is the Creator and He knows His creation.

"I will praise thee; for I am fearfully and wonderfully made: marvellous are thy works; and that my soul knoweth right well" (Psalm 139:14). When you step in, you rob God of His glory. You not only rob God, but you rob the world of who you really are. There is only one you.

CHAPTER 7

The Process of Exchange Begins

Many people believe that Christians use their faith as an excuse not to take control of their own futures. They say we are coping out in deciding a destiny of prosperity on our own. Among many other things that they may say, I beg to differ. Being a Christian is a life-long commitment of self-sacrifice and service. Please consider this: everyone who claims to be a Christian is not a born-again, baptized, blood-washed believer. I'm not asking anyone to agree or disagree with me. What I do know is this; you cannot be a *true* Christian and stay the same.

No one is born in the natural and stays the same forever. Unless the baby dies as a baby, it may be justified but, even then, changes will take place. If you are living, you must grow! It's not an option. It is the same in the spiritual realm. You cannot be born again and stay the same. You will begin to see small changes soon after your conversion. A conversion is an action word that requires change. I don't believe that anyone has a conversion and is unaware of it. It is where X marks the spot. In other words, the experience should be a memorable one. If you ask a "sold-out Christian" what marked the spot for them, you will get a personal testimony of their experience, and the day is as clear as if it were yesterday.

When a woman is pregnant, whether she wants the baby to grow or not, it will develop on its own because it will naturally feed off her. If she chooses not to eat, the baby will still take what it needs from the mother. So, why would we think that someone as powerful as the Almighty Creator of all things would plant His spirit in us and not compel a change to come forth? It will draw strength from God. It is something that cannot be contained or hidden. Eventually, pregnancy will show forth and a baby will be birthed. Birth comes forth at an appointed time as the full evidence of what was growing inside of you.

I say all of this because Christianity gets a bad rap when we claim to be something that we are not. It's not that you cannot be; it's because you have not chosen to be. You may have grown up in church. Your auntie can be an evangelist and your daddy a pastor. That does not make you a Christian. There are too many people sitting in church doing the "church thing." That is not salvation. Salvation is a verbal confession with the mouth and the heart. Not your physical heart but your spiritual heart. Your heart *does* speak to God. You must know and understand that Jesus is Lord, and He sacrificed Himself for you. You must know that you need Him to come into your life. Then, you will be free and change will come. I hear people all the time say, "I grew up in church; I know God." "When I was a child, I got saved." "I know what I need to do; I pray all of the time." All of these statements may be true, but they may also be masking their lack of a relationship with Jesus.

The bottom line is, when you were in church did you really hear the words that were spoken? Then, you would know that God desires a personal relationship with each of us. Some of us will get to the gates of heaven, and Jesus will say depart because I don't know you (Luke 13:24–27). Jesus said it! So, I guess that settles it. Plain and simple, you cannot account for someone's credibility unless you personally know them and you are in relationship with them and in good standing.

Salvation means to be free. We should be free in all things. It doesn't mean that life will stop throwing us curve balls. It does mean, however, that you should learn the strategy of how the ball will be thrown and who is throwing it to avoid being hit and utterly knocked out every time. Catch the ball sometimes and throw it back at the enemy. You should not be in bondage forever and serving a master that keeps you in chains. The Bible says to know to do good and to choose not to do it is a sin (James 4:17). Good also means to know what is right in your doing.

You can't continue to know what is right and choose not to do it, and still say you are a Christian. It is the Holy Ghost's (the spirit of God) responsibility to prompt the heart of a Christian to right living and change. The Bible speaks of us being known by our fruit and that our fruit will reveal if we are of the devil or God. Praying to God is great, but if there is no action that follows, you are just talking. "Faith without works is dead" (James 2:20b). You may not like what I'm saying, but it's the truth and if you take heed, it may set you free. This is my desire and my prayer for you! Change will only come when we choose to take the steps. If you are thinking that I am asking you to question your salvation, I probably am. I'm just asking you to check yourself. Check your motives and intentions in your walk. Make sure you are in right standing and not religious standing. This may be your last opportunity.

My process of change was long, and many challenges surfaced along the way. Through it all, I was being rooted in truth, and change was bound to spring forth. It is important to stay in the process. The result will be greater than the pain you suffered.

By now, I felt totally confused in life. I decided to leave everyone alone for a couple of months. Then, I did something that seemed crazy even to me at that time. I went back to the boyfriend who cheated on me. As crazy as it seemed, I needed to stay put for a while. God changed my heart and turned it to Himself. No, I didn't run back to church and fall on the altar to give my life to the Lord. Not yet.

I learned that standing still can become your place of strength. I believe God planted my feet long enough to settle my spirit. Before, I was good at just running to the next relationship. When you are constantly moving, you cannot clearly see or hear what is being done. For the first time ever, I found a sense of peace in this settled place. I had gone back to my last boyfriend and stayed with him for the next three years. It was still a lot of drama from both of us. The one thing I knew was that if it were not for the experience of him cheating on me, I would not have seen what I was doing to others and myself. I continually thanked him for that experience. He always thought I was throwing the past in his face. He didn't understand that I was really sincere. You would have to stand in the light to see the beauty of how God was working things out through my pain.

I suffered many things in that relationship, even rape. You may be thinking, *How is that so, you were dating him?* Yes, I was. The bottom line is rape is a violent display of control over another human being (by force) in the form of a sexual act. Dating or not it's still rape and it really shook me. After it was over, he simply said that he was getting ready to go to church, as if nothing had just happened. I was in shock with all that had taken place. I got up without a word and went home.

I had never felt so dirty in my life. I remember getting in the shower and just crying. I just kept washing and trying to wash away the dirt and filth and I couldn't. You would think that I wouldn't have reacted that way seeing that at other times I was giving myself to him freely. When you are violated in that way, it doesn't matter whether you know the person or not. It is a violation of your humanness and that's putting it mildly. I stopped seeing him for about three months. I asked him to stay away from me. I made it very clear that this was rape. It was so degrading that I chose not to tell anyone. I was mortified!

After much talking, we got back together. As always, things were okay for a period of time, and then all of the drama started again. I must say, most of the drama came from me. I was probably one of the most unstable chicks anyone knew, but it was all covered up with goodness and a smile. I wanted to do right. I just didn't know how. It would truly take the work of God to teach me about life and how to be a goodly, and godly, woman.

I decided that, once again, I would leave for good (what I thought would be for good). Almost two months had passed, and he was starting to leave me alone. I had not slept with anyone, so I was doing well. I had gone to the clinic because I had to have some tests taken. I had not been feeling well. The clinic told me to come back in. I knew something was not right. They asked if I could be pregnant. I told them there was no way. I had not been with anyone in two months. To rule out everything, I took the test for their sake. I found out that the last time I slept with him I got pregnant. I had been dating this guy for three years. Why now? I was floored! I knew I would be trapped. With this news, I would be tied forever to a crazy, out-of-control, jealous baby daddy. I was trying to get away from him, not stay with him. I did not want to have this baby, but I knew that I had promised God many years before that I would never have another abortion.

Yes, I did say *another*. I am telling this not because I condone abortions by any means. I know that many women have found themselves in this position before. They made the same choice that I did for whatever reason. There is nothing right about taking a life that is a part of you. Children are truly a gift from God and to this world. I took away a part of our history that can never be replaced. We don't know what their assignment could have been. They could have been world changers, cure finders, or famous inventors. Whatever they were supposed to be, we took away their destiny. There are women who have had mental meltdowns or breakdowns over this. I became one of them.

I want you to know that God is a forgiving and a merciful God. Once we give it to Him, He moves forward. Sometimes it is harder for us to forgive ourselves. You cannot change what you have done. If you let go of it and give it to God, He will heal you and make you a testimony for another woman. He is an expert at doing that. These things are not easy to say, but they are necessary. I will leave no stone unturned as I move forward in my victory. When you leave hidden secrets, you give the enemy a stone to cast at your glass house. Live in a glass house, but leave no stones behind. Fortify your glass with truth. Fragments of these thrown stones may scratch the surface, but they will not penetrate the product.

It was such a shock that when I left the clinic the doctor gave me a card to call someone for counseling. A few days later, I called and told him. I found myself sick with morning sickness from the time I told him. I had never experienced morning sickness with any of the other pregnancies. I was sick twenty-four hours a day. I was miserable. About two months had passed. Everything was well.

Out of nowhere, he decided to leave town without my knowledge. Two days later when I got in touch with him, he explained to me that he had left town and he would be back in a few days. He said he had gone to see a sick friend. I knew what he told me was a lie or at least not all of the truth. I flipped out. Although I had changed in the area of cheating, he had not and I could not go through it again. I felt like, *If you are going to do this, let's be on equal playing grounds. Don't do it when I'm in a vulnerable position like pregnancy.* I would not have cheated on him. I would have left him and, once again, showed him how the game was to be played at its best. I was no joke back then. I was truly a force to be reckoned with and not in a good way. Without any thought or prayer, I made an appointment at the abortion clinic and did the very thing I vowed never to do . . . again. I had not even given myself twelve hours to think about this life-altering decision that I was about to make. The morning sickness stopped immediately, but the sickness in my mind and spirit of what I had done sent me into an instant depression. This was different from the past experiences I had. There was never an emotional attachment to my past decisions. I could not even get out of bed because I was so depressed. The absence of the life that was growing inside of me affected me more than I could ever express. You see, when I had the first abortion, the clinic explained to me that early on in pregnancy, it's not really a baby. It's a blob of tissue. It had no life or form attached to it. If you find yourself in this situation, don't believe the lie. It has form and a heartbeat usually before you ever find out it was planted in the womb. It is alive and has nerve endings throughout. That means, it feels everything; including its departure from the womb.

When my boyfriend returned from out of town, he was devastated by the news. It was days before Mother's Day. I dreaded that day when it came. This would have been his first child, and he had told everyone how much he was looking forward to having this baby. I had already told everyone that I was having another baby also. Now, I would have to make up something about the pregnancy. I told everyone I had a miscarriage. It's not something you pride yourself in by freely sharing when you have taken a life. I was hurting so much that I found myself trying to get pregnant again, but it didn't happen. It made a hole in my soul that was left unfilled. Eventually, we finally broke up. A few months later, I found myself in the next relationship. When you don't know what to do, you will do what you know.

This was my way of getting over the last relationship (not really get over because I didn't get over, I suppressed, covered up, and moved forward). I must say, he did treat me well. I only needed to ask for what I wanted or tell him where I wanted to go and it was done. He gave me the seed money that I needed to start a business. He took me to all of the business appointments I needed to go to when I didn't feel like driving. He was "hooking a sister up" in other ways, and he was a great cook. He was not overbearing, and his mannerism was awesome. When we were together, his attention was totally on me. His attention was so on me that I failed to see that it was not on my children. My children and I are a package deal. I spent time with my children and continued to be the attentive mother I had always been. He was truly there for me and me alone. I only see that now in hindsight. They say hindsight is 20/20 vision. My feelings and intentions may sound confusing and contradictory, but it's not. Many times, when you are going through a process, you are confused and your actions look like they are contradictory. You go back and forth until you figure out which direction is the right direction. It's like when you are on a road, lost. You will continue to go back to the same starting point of where you lost sight of your direction. You will keep turning around again until you see a new landmark located in the direction you are supposed to be going.

After being romanced by him for a year, I was pregnant again. No, it was not an accident. I did nothing to prevent it and neither did he. I was trying to get closure from the past, and he knew it. That's not an excuse. It's the truth. What his excuse was, I could not tell you. When I brought the news to him, he seemed shocked. That really upset me. Just before I found out I was pregnant, God showed me in a dream that I would be having another baby. I did share that with him. He showed no emotion other than joy. We got off to a rocky start, but things smoothed out along the way. My boyfriend was there to make sure my needs were met, and I had a sense of peace about it all.

When I was about four months along, I had a vision that this baby would be a boy. I could see my sister, from whom I was estranged, playing with my baby. Suddenly, someone walked past me, but when he did, it was like he was walking through me. There was a shadow-type spirit being standing beside me.

Instantly, I was aware that I was not in my physical body. I then blurted out, "Oh my God, am I dead?" There was no answer, but I knew I was in the presence of God. With desperation, I began to plead with God. I said, "Please don't leave me here. I want to be with You. Take me with You. Don't leave me." As I pleaded, I felt myself move quickly through space and time into darkness. Then I entered into a cold place, and I felt myself return to my body. I was moving at what felt like the speed of light and three distinct dimensions. Then, my eyes opened. It wasn't like waking up. I just opened my eyes.

I was excited about the experience of seeing my son. Just the thought of being in the presence of God was pleasing to me. At that time, I was not thinking about salvation. I thank God that He was. My first thought was, *This is a good dream*. My thoughts quickly turned to what I saw as a major problem. The problem was that it was my baby, my family, and me in this vision. His father was not there. This is not the dream that you want to have when you are pregnant and the person missing in the dream is sleeping right beside you. I woke him up and told him all about the dream. I let him know that we were having a son and the details of his features. I let him know that he was not there in my dream. I wanted an answer as to why he wasn't, and I was serious. Needless to say, I did not get an answer or much comfort from that dream. I didn't talk about it anymore. I tucked it away in my heart and watched the events unfold in my life.

God had begun to deal with me frequently in these night visions. He would show me other people in my life, events to come, and myself. I believe that when God gives dreams, they can be literal or symbolic. If He does not clarify them for you, don't try to figure it out. The thoughts of God cannot be figured out. "For as the heavens are higher than the earth, so are my ways higher than your ways, and my thoughts than your thoughts" (Isaiah 55:9). Only God can reveal them to you in His time.

During this time, He also showed me that I would be a minister or some sort of shepherd. I could see myself speaking before forums of women. I did not understand how He would do that because I had already said I would never be a part of a church again. I really felt like church folk were all hypocrites. My experience had taught me not to trust leadership. Every religious person I knew at that time was the image of the world in a suit or fancy dress with a hat. There was no difference between the two. The church community was a family of said believers with most of them going straight to hell. Their actions would cause anyone to fall. Their behavior did not line up with the Word of God. Once God started changing my heart, I could no longer accept the saints doing whatever they wanted. I did not see that I, too, was being hypocritical with my lifestyle. I began to condemn them as I was convicted about their behavior. I would confront the behavior and make it known that they were no different from me. They could not debate the facts of my truth. My self-righteous attitude was overbearing, but those who carried the label had nothing to fight with.

Dreams are a powerful and revelatory way that God sometimes chooses to communicate with His people. If taken seriously, you will have insider information that others around you may not be privy to. I recommend you write your dreams down. Dreams and visions are different. So I encourage you not to throw away all of them. It could be God trying to talk to you about your destiny, and it validates the importance of your communication with Him. God does not deal with everyone in the same way. My experiences may never be yours. Thankfully, we don't need each other's endorsements or validation. We only need God's.

Demons?

With this third pregnancy, I began to desire a relationship with God. I began to know Him in ways I had never imagined Him working. My heart was reaching for His heart. My desired a relationship with this mighty, powerful, and loving God that I was becoming familiar with. No one ever expressed to me that He would be my friend, father, lawyer, provider, and anything else I needed Him to be. I was elated by even the thought of Him. I knew I was tapping into something that others around me were not familiar with. I would walk into a room with a giant smile on my face. People couldn't understand why I was so happy.

There was also a downside to all of this. I began to have supernatural experiences. What I will talk about in a minute is not for the critics or the psychologically impaired judges. Judgment will only keep you in ignorance. New information should be explored before thrown to the side. Examine the physical things with the things that the eyes can perceive. The spiritual things can only be understood through a spiritual encounter. I won't wish this for you, but I am here to share with you a realm that you may not be familiar with. Be open to hear.

During my fifth month of pregnancy, things started to change. What I didn't realize is that when you turn to God, the enemy is never far behind trying to win you back. He will do his best to torment you, confuse you, and make you turn away from God. I began to have spiritual experiences that no one told me existed. I don't need medication. It may sound like it, but this information could save your life or someone else's. If you take it serious enough, you will understand your own life better. There is a spiritual world and it's very real. I pray that you will be open to what I have to say whether you understand it or not.

Aside from the dreams that God had been showing me about things that would soon happen, I began to experience demonic encounters. You may be asking, "What does that mean?"

It is when the spiritual world begins to impact the natural or physical world we live in. Just as there are angels in the spiritual realm, there are demons as well. These spirit beings are evil, and they only want to do harm. Their plans are always for your destruction. The Bible says, "The thief cometh not, but for to steal, and to kill, and to destroy: I am come that they might have life, and that they might have it more abundantly" (John 10:10). The "thief" is Satan, and the demons work for him. We all have a spirit that lives inside this physical body. You cannot see it, but trust me it's there. It has been labeled as many things (Aura, Chi, Life Force, Inner Self, etc.). No matter what you call it, it's still your spirit. I am not implying that your spirit is demonic. I pray it isn't. If it is, keep reading. The blood of Jesus will take care of that.

When you are asleep, you are unaware of the activity of you spirit. Individuals have reported having experiences where they saw their own bodies lying dead or on an operating table. Others have accounted for being in places like meetings or events that were taking place and could give a full account on what took place, although they were not physically there. This is a spiritual encounter where your spirit will leave your body and go to another place. You may not believe it, but if you ever have one of these encounters, you will no longer be able to justify your unbelief.

For a time, I was having so many of these spiritual episodes that I was afraid to go to sleep at night. My spirit was at war with these demonic forces. I did not understand it then. It was so intense it caused me to cry out to God for help. Some of these encounters manifested physically on my body. Some mornings I woke up with long scratches on my back and arms. I knew I could not reach that far. I can't give you details, but I can tell you it was torture. One night I just could not fight any more. I cried out to God for help.

One night I clearly heard a demonic voice. It said, "I want your soul and your baby's soul." For some reason, it didn't scare me; it made me angry. I said, "You can't have my soul or my baby's soul! We belong to God, and you can't do anything to hurt us!" I don't know where that boldness came from, but it was there. After that night, I knew I had the victory over those evil spirits that had previously tortured me.

My confidence in God was being built daily. The tormenting spirits didn't stop, but now I had confidence from within. Many times, I found myself waking up quoting scriptures that I did not even know I knew. The Bible says, "Train up a child in the way he should go: and when he is old, he will not depart from it" (Proverbs 22:6). Whatever you deposit into your children when they are young, you will get a return on it later, good or bad.

I have heard stories told of big, beautiful, angelic beings. I don't discount their encounters. I have had enough of my own to know better than to do that. I will tell you that this is not my story. The angels I saw in my room one night during these encounters were huge in stature and in height. I saw the face of an eagle on one of them. The eyes were so piercing, my spirit leaped out of my body and made a dash for the exit.

The Bible speaks of episodes when prophets and priests from days of old saw these angels, they would fall on their face in fear of their presence. I kid you not; I went to make a dash for the door, and my spirit moved quicker than my body. At that time, something gently swept me up and laid me on the bed, and a peace that I had never experienced before fell upon me. I knew at that point that God had sent these angelic beings to watch over me and protect me. I knew they were ancient beings and warriors. They were not just white; they had colors of blue, red, yellow, etc. on them. I can't tell you what the other one looked like, but I'm sure there were more. That night ended my fight with these demonic forces for the rest of my pregnancy.

Although God's victory reigned from that night until this day, I still pray to God to never show me the face of these beings while I am living. My fear of demons ended that night, and my new fear of these angelic beings began. The Lord is still working on me in this area. He does not want us to be afraid of anything. Be careful of the experiences that you may be asking God for; you may get one of these.

This is a little note to the doctors, therapists, and counselors. Not everyone who is claiming to see demons and having talks with God is in need of medication. Not all people who walk down the street looking like they are talking to themselves need to be committed. Some people really have tapped into a spiritual realm they are unfamiliar with. No one locks up the person who reads palms and crystal balls. I see public advertisement for all kinds of "spiritual workings." These are legal jobs, and some of you are paying for the service. What if most of the people suffering from mental illness are really people who suffer from real demonic attacks? Medication or solitary confinement will not free them from their torment. I am not saying that this is so for your clients. It's just something to think about.

By the time I was thirty weeks pregnant, I had decided I did not want to continue in this relationship with my boyfriend. There was nothing wrong between us, but things were not right for me. We had a child on the way and the end of our relationship did not change my responsibility as a mother or his as a father. We just would not be together. I wasn't upset or angry. I just needed to begin to take control of my own life. Little did I know that he would not only separate himself from me, but also our son.

Five weeks later, my third son was born. He was five weeks early. When my son's father showed up at the hospital that evening, my family and friends ran him away. They let him know that there was no need for him to be there. That was my mistake. I should have stepped in and put a stop to what was going on, but I didn't. Ladies, if a man is halfway stable, in his right mind, and he's your child's father, you don't have the right to take that experience from him of seeing his child being born. You had the choice when you lay down with him. Once you are pregnant, it's no longer your choice. This has nothing to do with sticking up for him. It's about standing for what is right. For the next few weeks, my baby's father was around. He would stop by and spend time with our son, and he would babysit while I went to meetings and ran errands. He followed up to make sure that I was okay and did not need anything. Before long, however, he stopped coming altogether.

By the time my son became a teenager, he had only seen his father, in passing, one time. Even today, his father refuses to have a relationship with him. As a mother it hurt me. But I had to give this situation over to God. I have put this situation to rest. As a mother, it is a great burden to carry. Our children are our babies. When we see them hurt, we want to hurt somebody!

CHAPTER 8

Strength from Within

My mother and I were very close. Regardless of the things that happened to me as a child, I knew without any doubt that my mother loved me with all that she was. Once I became a mother myself, we grew closer. Although she was my mother, there was now common ground between us. We had become best friends. My mother respected me as a mother, a confidant, a friend, and her daughter. She confided in me some of her deepest hurts and pains. She knew she could vent with me and it would be safe. My mother meant so much to me. We travelled together, shopped, went out to eat, fished, and just hung out. She really was my best friend. I could not say enough about our relationship to express the uniqueness of it.

There had come a time when I had to confront my mother. Over the years, I kept having flashes of the bloody underwear and the beatings as a child. I had no other memory of the offense, so I kept putting it off. I went to therapy and still could not get to the bottom of this issue. With so much confusion within, I finally asked her if I was sexually abused. My mother was shocked that I would even remember. It had been so long ago, and over the years, I never even hinted at any awareness of this violation.

I became very upset after our discussion. The memories of the sexual abuse started coming back. I felt that she should have done so much more toward my offender. There were so many questions without answers. This new information began to shake my very foundation. Confusion was like a plague to my memory. In a short time, I became mad and almost disrespectful toward my mother. I told her she should have reported it to the police and exposed the perpetrator for the violence that would cause me to question everything I knew. I quickly was becoming unraveled.

I had a decision to make. Either I could point the finger and become bitter about what had already happened, or I could forgive the acts of neglect and abuse and continue this relationship that was now in jeopardy. I knew I could not change anything. I could choose to be mad for a very long time, but that would not make a difference. The fact was that my mother loved me and would never intentionally allow anyone to hurt me, or any of her children. With a lack of resources at hand, shame and guilt were there to compound this situation. She told me she didn't know what else to do. So, I chose to forgive her and let it go. I believe we became even closer after that. It brought a sense of closure to her and comfort to me to make peace with this information. I released her and moved on the best way I knew how.

We all make mistakes in life. If someone has forgiven you, then you too should forgive. If you want complete healing, you will have to forgive even your abuser. I had to do that. It was forty long years after the violation of my body and soul that I would fully be able to release the offense. It was suppressed so deeply in my subconscious that it would take God to work through layers of debris before getting to the root of it all. It had to be a God thing!

One morning I woke up and I heard in my spirit, "You have walked around this mountain forty years and that's long enough." All of the flashes of the past memories that plagued me for years were revealed in a moment of time. I had accepted a truth that I had not completely known up until that time. When the truth was revealed, I wept for the little girl inside. She had been robbed of her innocence, childhood, trust, peace, and joy. After the tears flowed, I embraced that scared little girl who had lost so much. I let her know that it was okay now. She did not have to be afraid anymore because I was there to take care of her, and there was safety in my arms. A soul integration was taking place. Some of these experiences may not be fully understood by someone who has not experienced extremely traumatic events that caused a separation of one's self. It is real and it does happen.

When I could cry no more tears, I then declared war on the enemy just as he declared war on me when I was young and innocent.

I declared that on my watch, he would not continue to destroy the minds and souls of innocent children and corrupt the expectancy of hopeful adults. I was, and am, committed to stand in the gap for them. I will not stand idly by while others mourn their losses of hopes and dreams for the future. I declare that we will all prosper and succeed to the fullest.

In fighting the battle, we must first look at some things. Sometimes we become angry with people about the things they are doing to themselves, others, and us. The truth is, until we understand the game plan and planner behind it all, we will lose the fight. The enemy is out to destroy you and everything connected to you. Be aware that he is always on the prowl looking for his next victim. Don't let his next victim be you. We do have the power to prevent many things. In order to do that, you must first be mindful that something is happening. It may be with you, your children, your loved ones, or others around you. Don't close your eyes to what could be happening right in front of you.

Something had to have happened to that teenaged boy for him to prey on me (and probably others) the way he did. I believe he had to have been the victim of someone else's abuse, which caused him to act out. I wept not only for myself but also for the other little girls who have never told their story. I cried for all those who did not have the opportunity to speak because their voices had been silenced. I mourned for the woman who was still caged in her own thoughts. Then, without a thought, I just said, "I forgive you." I forgave my perpetrator. It was a choice, but was it really? If I truly wanted to be free, it was not a choice. When you give yourself the opportunity not to forgive, you open the door to the possibility of a long struggle of constantly reclaiming the act of abuse. It will stay with you until you let go of it.

Forgiveness is a heart issue. As I said before, forgiveness is for you. It is a gift that you give to yourself. It allows you to be free from the hurt and pain that others have afflicted upon you. It is your declaration that no weapon formed against you will ever prosper (Isaiah 54:17). It takes more work to hold on to all of that weight than to release it. Unforgiveness will build a stronghold in your mind, and it will keep control over your thoughts, feelings, and emotions. It leaves space for fear and other things to creep in.

When I think about the power that I am still giving to someone who has caused me great pain, there is no other choice but to forgive. It is done by choice. When you choose to forgive, God comes in like an eraser to your soul and spirit and removes the emotional damage that has caused erosion over the years. You don't forget that it happened. It just no longer takes authority over your mental and emotional status. The thought of it will feel like it happened to someone else, but you know it was you. That's a great thing! God will prepare you to give of yourself and to give support to others in ways you would never have been able to before.

Have you ever shared what you were going through with a friend? By sharing, you had hoped to get some constructive feedback. Before the conversation was over, however, she told you all about herself and what *she* was going through. You didn't get the sense that she was telling you her story as an encouragement to you or to let you know you're not alone. You felt it was really more to "one-up" you. When the conversation was over, you were worn out and mad about life because what happened to her was so unfair. You feel hopeless for happiness. After enough of these conversations, you will begin screening your phone calls. You know if you pick up that phone, it will cost you what you are not willing to pay at this time. You say, not today!

You have just encountered a sister that is rusting away in her situation, and she doesn't even know it. She thinks she will help you by lending an ear. In reality, she can't really help anyone until she gets help for herself. After time and recovery, then she can be a shoulder to lean on. Until then, she is not the one for you to dump on. It doesn't matter how old she is; she needs maturing in her emotions and spirit. Continue to pray for her, but you must find yourself another confidant.

It was during these times that God covered me. He worked on my heart and placed great compassion in it. After having my third son, my relationship with God changed. It really intensified. I began to have the desire to feed the hungry, clothe the poor, and attend to the needs of those less fortunate than me. My family gave out Christmas and Thanksgiving baskets to needy families. I was financially poor but blessed, and I shared those blessings with others. I started listening to only gospel music, and all I talked about was the goodness of the Lord.

All of these changes had been going on inside of me since I asked Him to change me. It was a slow process. He worked it out so smoothly that I did not even notice when the changes took place.

I remember one Christmas taking all of the toys and wrapping them with the intentions of giving them away. My children and I took them to a shelter for homeless families. It became a tradition over the next couple of years. I remember the first year we did this. I had told my sons that we were not celebrating Christmas with toys; we were going to donate them. My oldest son didn't say anything. A week before Christmas, I pulled out all of the things I had bought and I said to them, "It's time to wrap the gifts." My son thought, *She must be out of her mind. I thought she was joking! I am not wrapping my gifts to give to somebody else. She must be crazy.* He was too upset with me (he later told me this).

Settling into my new life, I felt hopeful about the future. Until about two months after giving birth to my third son, I found out that my mother had breast cancer. It was a shock to the whole family. I had already begun to put up walls to block my emotions. I was no longer interested in being in a relationship with anyone other than myself. I was ready for change, but this was too much to consider at this time. The thought of a life-threatening disease attacking my mother's body was unthinkable. I decided not to think about any possibility of this becoming more serious than what it already was. I felt like I needed a dramatic physical change to match my internal resistance. I decided to cut my hair and grow dreadlocks. I stopped wearing makeup and only wore loose-fitting clothes. This may not seem like much to you, but for me, it was a 180-degree turn. I was quickly turning into my shell like a threatened snail.

I had not realized the impact all of this was having on me. The rejection from my last relationship had sent me into a tailspin. I could deal with someone rejecting me, but when it was my child being rejected, that was a different story altogether.

It became personal! I went into total rebellion with the male species. I felt the need to prove to them that there was more to me than what met the eyes. Because my baby and I were one, someone needed to be held responsible for the cruel acts that my child would be exposed to. I had already learned that it was easier to punish the one who could never leave you. So, punishing me was just what I did. Punishing myself was my way of expressing my frustration with the choices I had made. I could not punish anyone else for my decisions. It was not their fault I had become someone who did not like or respect herself enough to care about the whole person. I was angry for allowing my body to be used by men for their personal pleasure only. I was stuck in a box with no way out.

I was already very verbally abusive in my relationships with men and my children. This was my expression of disappointment in my lack of understanding of why I did the things I did. This confusion always brought sadness to my soul. Although I was unaware of the reasoning behind my madness, I believe that the anger with my children was the expectancy of them growing up and doing the same thing to women that was being done to me. I know it sounds crazy, but I believe it is true. The physical traits that drew men to me were used as a weapon against me. They were the only weapons I knew of and I used them. Somehow, I thought I would get different results one day. I know now that it was insanity!

I needed someone to see me as more than just a pretty face or nice body or just well put together. I was more than hair, boobs, and a butt. What I had been putting out was exactly what I was getting back, and I was tired of the results. Three children later, a failed marriage, and the image of being dynamite in the bedroom was not what I had dreamed for myself. I had an infant, a preteen, and an out-of-control teenager at the time. I wanted and needed more than anyone was able to offer me. Going through hell was not where I was at; I was stuck in hell unaware. Seriously!

I spent the next year and a half of my life with just my children and me. I walked with a look on my face that said, "Don't even think about it. I will hurt you!" I boldly wore my tattoo of a cobra in a striking position with his tail wrapped around a red rose. I was so proud when someone would ask me what it was.

I didn't just tell them; I justified the nature of its existence. I was angry, bitter, and the source of my own suffering. Those who walked away from me may have scarred me, but I nursed those wounds with the poison of my past to promote a deadly infectious disease ("dis" "ease"). I was comfortable in the hallways of despair.

A year and a half should not be long enough to forget your history of patterns of self-destruction. You would think that I would have learned by now. No, not me! That would be way too easy. At first, I rejected all men. But after a while, I began to date again. I was introduced to a guy through a friend. One evening, I let myself go too far with him. I heard a voice in my ear as if someone else was right there in the room with us. The voice said, "Don't do it!" However, two years after deciding not to give myself to anyone, I, once again, compromised my mind, body, and spirit. I was forewarned and did it anyway. One of the things I have not spoken much about is the fear of being rejected. Fear of rejection is a major issue for many women. You may not currently identify with this issue, but it is lurking behind a lot of unidentified actions. Up until this point, I didn't have any idea of why I compromised so much. I understood that my life and health was on the line every time I chose to have intercourse. I was well aware of pregnancy, disease, and mental torment over poor choices. Somehow, it was never enough to stop me from this destructive behavior. It just didn't make any sense as I racked my brain over the years. Someone with rejection issues know the crazy reasons why they do what they do. It may not make sense to others. In a moment of decision making, it is safe and that is what is important to them.

My fear of rejection represented the fear of being pushed away from the love of a father. I felt that I needed someone to say, "You are enough for me; I accept you as you are." As a woman, I looked for my lover to give me what only a father can give. All little girls need that from their fathers. There are no real substitutes. It is devastating mentally and emotionally when she does not get that validation. The relationship between a father and daughter lays the foundation of teaching self-value and how she is to be treated in intimate relationships. Without that, she imagines what it should look like, and it's usually a fairy tale.

Many women have grown up without fathers. Many of them (not all) find themselves in this situation, and they never figured out the dysfunction of their actions. They know there is a problem with what they are doing, but they usually don't get to the root of it. As I said before, what we don't get as a child we will seek as an adult. It was that same fear of rejection that stopped me from getting off that bed and walking out the door. It was all for a moment of acceptance! What a price to pay for a lie.

About three days after my sexual encounter, while driving, I saw a flash before my eyes. God showed me that I was pregnant again. *No! That can't be right. I don't even like this guy!* At that time, my youngest son was less than two years old. I did not want or need another child. I was happy with what I had.

The weight of the world quickly fell upon my shoulders. I kept saying, "Please, God, don't let this be true." But I knew it was true. I told the guy I was pregnant and he ran (figuratively) in the other direction. I had no strength or desire to chase him down and prove my case. I was (felt) trapped and needed a way out. I couldn't blame him for feeling like this was not his child, and I was trying to set him up. Who knows, if one of my boys said that he was in a similar situation as this before I personally experienced it, I probably would have told him, "It's not yours." Since it has happened to me, I know it's possible, and my advice would be to them: consider the possibility. I was so embarrassed, ashamed, and guilt stricken. I couldn't tell anyone. I felt like every bad thing that was ever spoken about me was true. It did not matter that I had changed in a lot of areas. I had no longer set out to hurt others. I was living the best life I knew how, and I felt good about that. But the bottom line was my actions took me on a road with a great price attached to it. The burden was more than I could bear.

This really took me for a loop. I had already been left to raise my last child alone. I had not even dated since I was pregnant with my third son. I kept praying that God would understand this situation and give me the go ahead to abort this pregnancy.

God does not give us the authority to be Him. He is the giver of life, and it's never the right choice to take a life. I had made wrong decisions in the past, but I could not travel that road again. I prayed to have a miscarriage. I begged and pleaded with God. Finally, I heard God say, "You will have this baby, and he will be yours." A peace can over me, and I knew what I had to do. I had to go through with this pregnancy. Until now, I hadn't even taken a pregnancy test. That's how sure I was. However, I made it official. I took the pregnancy test; it was positive.

Transitions

At this point, you may be asking, "Where is the evangelist in this story?" For everything there is a season and a time for all things to manifest (Ecclesiastes 3:1). This book is about the process of the journey to becoming what I was always supposed to be. Continue reading and you will find that it was all a part of the intricate weaving of a perfect plan. It was a master plan in the Master's hands.

Now that I had made it official with the pregnancy test, I shared this news with my mother. After verbally expressing her disappointment, she had wanted to know if I had lost my mind. One thing about my mother was she never had a problem with speaking her mind. If she did not like something or someone, you knew it. It took a couple of weeks for her to get used to the idea. She became a great source of support to me after that.

She was an ear to hear my cries without judgment. She protected me from the naysayers who were out to discredit the reputation I had held on to for so long. At this point, it was all I had left. She did not allow anyone to dismiss the importance of her new grandchild who was soon to come.

Seeing the condition I was in, she knew this was not the time to pressure me about anything. I was so depressed. Doom covered me like a plague. If I had not had the responsibility of having a little one to fully depend on me, I'm not sure if I would have made it through my mother's illness. God surely walked through this process with me. I don't know if you have ever been in a situation that would cause you to have to look up. By yourself, you have no strength. The God that I had not known much about up to this point had to show up. I knew *of* Him, but not about Him. Regardless of the support system I had, it was not enough to pull me out of this place of despair. I felt like my foundation was quickly slipping from under me. I had not realized that my foundation had already begun to be built on my Lord and Savior, Jesus Christ. This foundation is a solid rock. Trust me on this one!

I had no money to provide for this child. My disobedience to the voice I had heard before the encounter that landed me in this situation was more than I could bear. Although God said that this child would be mine, I decided to seek out adoption. A friend and his wife, who lived in another state, offered to raise my child with no strings attached. I was humbled at his offer. It was a perfect plan for me. I did not want to have anything around me to remind me of the fall I had taken. I took them up on their offer. My mother thought, *Surely, she has lost her mind now!* She said, "I will not let you do that. I will take this child myself and raise it." After a few arguments about it, she finally left it alone. At least openly she did.

When I was four months pregnant, I went to church with a fraternal organization I had been a part of; it was part of my obligation to the organization. I will never forget the message that was preached that day. The preacher was speaking about separating yourself from among the crowd. He spoke about being willing to be holy, as God was a holy God. The words rang through me as if I were the only one hearing them. God was asking the people who in this crowd would be willing to commit themselves to Him and live holy before Him.

I knew God was calling me to come to Him. With no hope in sight and nothing to lose, I answered the call that day in my heart—I asked Jesus to come into my life and be Lord and Savior over it. I thought, *Things have got to get better because they can't get any worse.* Or so I thought. (I did not know at that time that you must lose *all* of you to take on all of Him.) It had been twelve long years since I had been connected to a religious institution. I knew I needed to be connected in fellowship with others who believed as I did. Soon after, I found a church home. It was a small membership, but the presence of God in that place was unmistakable. After a few visits, I knew I had found my new church home. It wasn't anything special that someone said or did. It was not the choir or some wonderful soloist who grabbed my attention. I just knew it was where I was supposed to be.

During this pregnancy, my mother's health took a turn for the worse. The cancer had spread throughout her whole body, and it was quickly taking a toll on her. Her energy level was very low. I would talk to her on the phone a couple of times a day to keep her connected to what was happening with her grandchildren and me. Many people could not understand the closeness of our relationship. As with all relationships, it takes a lot of time and commitment to one another. Yes, she was my mother, but I invested myself through selfless acts of love and kindness that she had not experienced from anyone else. When I hear the grumbles of how my mother was closer to me than anyone else, it is bothersome. What they don't realize is that I sacrificed a large part of myself and what I wanted in order to give space in my life to fulfill her wants and needs. No one else was willing to do that so no one else received that. The building of any good relationship takes time and consistency. You cannot get what others have if you are not willing to pay the price that others pay. These things don't come for free!

Eight months into my pregnancy, we almost lost her. I was under a lot of pressure during this pregnancy. I was with my mother every day. I lived about a half hour from her house. I didn't mind the ride. It was just as important for me to be there for her as it was to her. When unconditional love walks in the room, nothing else is an option. I didn't allow anything to get in the way of me not being there for her. Having her grandchildren and me there daily was the strength she needed to run that race a little while longer. It was an honor to serve my mother.

One day my mom needed me to go to the store for her. As I was getting out of my van, the inner seam of my pant leg ripped. It was a very large rip. I had to make a decision whether I was going to go into the store with this big hole in my pants or go back home and change. It would have taken me forty-five minutes to get to my house from the store and forty-five minutes to return. I decided I would just run in the store, grab what she needed, and head back to her house. As soon as I got in the store and headed down the aisle, I heard voices behind me talking and laughing. One of them said, "She knows things aren't *that* bad. She could have worn something better than that." After a few other remarks, I turned down the next aisle. I had never been so humiliated in my life. I was too ashamed to even turn around and respond or even see their faces. I was already embarrassed having to make a decision to go into the store to start with. It was one of the most degrading moments in my life, and they were unaware. I was beat down from this pregnancy that burdened my soul. My mother was lying sick, close to death, and it was ninety degrees outside. Those words crushed me, but at the same time, something rose up in me. I thought, *They don't know who I am or what my situation is! How dare they judge me? They don't know if this is all I have to wear or not.* Something within me knew I was becoming something greater than my situation or what I looked like on the outside. Although I did not know what greater was at that time, I knew it was more than this. I said to myself, "Wait until God prospers me. Then they will see and know not to judge anyone anymore. Things happen!"

The lesson here is: don't judge anyone. You don't know their story. Even if you do, it doesn't give you the right to impress your opinions upon them. Not everyone will be able to walk away from this attack as I did. There is a world out there that is in pain and suffering. Don't be the one to shove them over the edge. The small things you do and say could be what shatters their glass house. Their blood will be accounted to you.

Many things along the way had taken place in order to get me to where I was. The account that I will share with you is the true beginning of my conversion. They were truly defining moments.

I had started attending church regularly, and I found myself weeping heavily at every service. At that time, I was quite laid back (it was a big thing for me to stand up and clap my hands a little) in praising God. Many of you can relate to that. I had figured out that I needed to be in all of the prayer lines. I stopped caring about what people were thinking about me being up there so much. I needed some help, and I was going to get it one way or another. I stood up for prayer and awaited my turn. As my pastor prayed for me, he laid his hand upon my head, and his wife laid her hands on my pregnant belly. When I opened up my mouth, shouts of praise erupted. Hallelujahs came bellowing out of my mouth, and it would not stop. Then I heard the voice I had heard eight months prior. It said, "Stop condemning this baby with your actions and your word. I have blessed you with life. I could have allowed you to contract a disease that would have killed you, but instead, I blessed you. Lift your head up from this moment on and love this child. Do not walk with your head held down any more."

In my heart, I was so full of hurt that I vowed not to love this child. I had wanted no part of the memory of my pain. The only thing I can say now is, "But God." God had not only a plan for my life; He had a plan for my son's life as well. After I heard His words, I wept irrepressibly. As the praise went forward, I felt something release out of the pit of my belly, and it came up out of my mouth. For the next twenty-four hours, my uterus contracted. I thought I was going into labor, but it stopped. Every time I thought about that experience over the next seven days, I wept uncontrollably. I could not even tell anyone my experience through my tears. That day, I walked away with a freedom I had never known before. I embraced my pregnancy and prepared for my baby to come into this world. I was full of joy, peace, and hope. I did not know how I was going to care for him, but I knew God was going to take care of all of us. He was a "new" God to me because I never knew Him in this way. I knew *of* Him, but I did not *know* Him. I instantly had a peace in my mind and my spirit that I did not know existed. Whatever was released no longer had a hold on me or my baby. I knew I had just encountered a supernatural event that marked a new beginning for me. Words cannot capture the power of that encounter.

My change came quick and dramatically. When people made comments about my pregnancy that were not positive, I would reply, "God has blessed me with this baby, and we will be all right." My mother was there to experience this event with me. She knew me well, so I did not have to explain that this was not just a show of emotions. She knew something real had taken place. As we left church that day, she said, "This baby is going to be blessed. He is special." After that, we rode home in silence as I continued to weep.

My fourth son was born a month later. He was healthy and looked just like my mother. That was amazing in itself because I don't look anything like my mother. During my pregnancy, my mother had a dream that this child would look just like her. She described him perfectly. I knew God had allowed her to see him just as I had seen my previous son before he was born. She was so excited! She was truly leaving her mark on this world in the form of a son being given to her.

My God is awesome. He knew that my mother would not be around to see this child grow to maturity. Although they had a short relationship, I believe it was the one that settled her. My mother was a second mother to all of her grandchildren. She protected them from everyone, even their own parents. You could not tell her that those children were not hers. God had showed her my baby in detail before he was born. It was moments like this that were considered to be precious gifts to enjoy during the time she had left. My mother passed away when my last son was six months old.

CHAPTER 9

Boxes Are Built for Breaking Out

This excerpt is from one of my expressive writings after the loss of my mother:

As I sit in my box, or what I feel like a box, the trash from others keeps building up. Having no energy to fight or even stand, I sit in the corner of my box. No one sees the box I am in and neither do they care to see. I receive the waste that has been stored up for my mother. All of the negativity that was bound for her has been loosed on me. I receive the bitterness that comes with the resentment from the close relationship that we share. I receive the anger and shock that has triggered the emotions in others due to her passing.

The world keeps spinning, and the trash keeps landing in my box of safety. It is my personal space. My box has no lid on it. I know there is a world out there because I hear them bustling by.

They are too busy to notice that a box is sitting in the middle of the road. My soul is too sick to muster up strength to scream or yell, "I'm in here!" A small squall of "help" resonates from out of my box. There is still no answer on the other side.

It brings a little comfort knowing that I can still look up. The sunsets are majestic and the sunrises are magical. Rainbows sometimes appear in the sky after the storm. It gives me hope for the greater that is to come. This is not the end of my story. That is the hope that I close my eyes to every night.

Not having a top on your box does come with its inconvenience. During the day, the sun gives heat, but at high noon, it's too hot. When it rains, I get wet. I am now wet and night falls. Cool and windy is the night air. My body temperature begins to fall. As the windstorms come, it drops more debris in my box. In time, the trash really piles up. I need a way out. I am here today not being able to relate to myself anymore. Not wanting to be in this box anymore. I want to feel again. I want to live again. I want to be free! No more reckless living, but free to live in the Lord. I just don't know how to get out of here. Should it take a lifetime to heal from past hurts? I don't think so! Maybe, just maybe, if I pile up all of this trash that has collected in my space, I'll have enough to lift me up out of this place.

I had placed myself in a box. My box was built for self-preservation. That box kept me from slipping away. I had chosen God to be my main source of strength. As I was riding down the road of life, I hit my first brick wall. This brick wall was the wall that represented rejection. I was broken from past hurts and pains of intimate relationships. I had decided that I won't share my emotions anymore. I poured my love and energy onto my children, but that part of me had shut down. So in reality, I was pouring out water just to get them wet. Like empty vessels of poison, I poured out my love. After having to face my mother's illness and support her in the way she needed me to, the second wall went up. I could not afford to feel. So I shut down another part of me. My third wall went up when I found myself in a situation that brought great self-condemnation, guilt, shame, and such embarrassment I did not want to be seen in public. It was the unexpected pregnancy. This one almost took me out. It was such a heavy weight to carry that I almost folded. The last went up when my mother passed from breast cancer. The loss was so great that in order for me to move forward, the fourth wall had to go up. I remember the following day after my mother passed I went to the facility where we were having a memorial service. I walked in the kitchen to thank everyone for helping. A flood of emotions had come over me, and I was about to succumb to them. In that moment, I spoke within myself and said, *You cannot fall apart right now. There is no one to pull you together if you do. Your children are depending on you and they have no one else.* And with those words, I completely shut down emotionally.

A whole year had passed before I would even allow myself to miss my mother and shed tears over the loss. It would take three years before I could grieve her death and completely mourn the loss. Her passing represented all that I knew a solid foundation to be. It was now gone in a sudden moment. With my mother, my friend, and my confidant gone, my whole support system melted away in one day.

I was now shut up in a box that prohibited me from giving or receiving love, compassion, sympathy, or any other emotion that required input from me. I was alone and emptied of the emotions that one would feel to indicate she is still alive. They were gone! In addition, I was the dumping ground for those who had also taken a hit from my mother's passing.

My grandmother stayed with me after my mother's passing for two months. She could not bring herself to leave and return home childless. The one person I thought could understand me was my maternal grandmother. We had a close relationship as well. She had lost her only child, and both of us were empty and hurting. We soon became the source of the other's discomfort. I believe that my grandmother took all of her frustration out on me because I was the closest person to my mother. She lashed out at me so much that I did not want to come home to my own house. It was very painful, and pain was quickly becoming all that I knew.

Sometimes the "box" that is meant to keep you locked in can be your reserve tank to catapult you into your destiny. As I said before, no one can stop your destiny but you. I wrote this at a critical time in my life. I was at a crossroad, and I did not know it. I was stuck in a box that I built, and I was the only one who knew where the escape hatch was located. When you are down, the only way out is up. Take the time to find out what is stored in your box. You may be surprised at what you may find. Under all of that debris, I bet there is an evacuation plan in the midst. What was meant to weigh you down can be used to your advantage. Know that while you are in your box, you are not alone. God will be there as long as you allow Him to be.

Through all of this, I cared for my children by myself. My youngest son was severely sick with asthma from the age of two months. Before my mother had passed, I remember my baby being hospitalized for asthma at four months old and my mother having surgery in the hospital next door. It was to be a last-ditch effort to clear her liquid-filled lungs before the doctors completely gave up. It was a last chance of hope to prolong her life, but it did not work. I still had a two-year-old and a teenager I was responsible for. That's not to mention my older teenager who was caught up in the things of the world that I was totally against. With my stress on overload, I ran back and forth between hospitals checking on my son and my mom. Most days, I ran on E. No gas in my energy tank and sometimes no gas in my car tank either. During this time, the child support that I was receiving had stopped coming for eight months. I had no money and no time to think about it. I had to be responsible. I had everyone depending on me.

I took responsibility for my babies, kept my mouth shut, and kept it moving. I became the buffer between my children and their fathers to protect them as much as I could. I wanted to talk, but I felt like no one really wanted to listen. Did they really care? That question nagged at me. I didn't know, and I didn't have time to figure it out. I had no time to stop to seek answers. Eventually, I closed the door to the world and stayed in my box where it was safe for me.

As alone as I may have felt, God always showed up to strengthen me at critical moments of desperation. My world seemed very dark. I kept reading the Word and going to church. I had nothing else. The glimmer of light that shone in the Bible was my place of hope. All of my available time was spent with my God. He had to be all that my mother was and more. Many people did not understand my worship or service to God. In reading this, maybe they will.

Earlier I mentioned that it took me twelve years to turn back to my Lord and Savior, Jesus. Through my suffering, I found the unending hope that resides throughout this book. I was carrying a weight that was never intended to be carried alone. You know that poem "Footprints in the Sand"? I tell people that for me, there were drag marks in the sand on that beach. Sometimes even in the midst of needing help, I fought the One Who had come to rescue me. I know He drug me out. I thank Him for the drags.

Cries from the Shadows of Darkness

This journal writing is expressive of my state of transitioning at the time:

Can anybody hear me? Can you hear the cries of my soul? It's ringing out from the darkness of my mind's thoughts and even my heart. The anguish of my burdens dig deeper and deeper until silence rings out in the stillness of the night of a rushed life.

Is there anybody there? Is there a hand to touch to bring comfort or a mouth to speak strength into my weakness? Oh how the saints hustle by with their religious suits painted on their faces. It's just a cover up for the hidden secrets that lay in the heart of a just man.

The scarlet letter adorns their heads. It's covered in beauty and displays righteousness, but all is not what it seems. Why should one suffer alone? There must be someone here who understands. Can you feel my pain? Can you bear witness to my testimony? The night is here and day is soon to come. There is hope in the dawning of a new day. Hope thou in God? Yes Lord, my hope is in You.

CHAPTER 10

Stay Focused on Your Focus

There is a place we have been praying to get to. As our prayers go forth, we feel like they still have not been answered. So we continue to wait. What we have failed to realize is that our prayers have already been answered, and we are standing in the midst of it. When you stay focused on your focus, you begin to see the big picture before you. You push past what you think you know and begin to focus on the ultimate goal of victory. However, it requires God's strength.

We have a tendency to keep our great big God in a box. When things don't look the way we think they ought to, we continue asking over and over again, expecting the manifestation of what has already manifested. We have eyes, but we cannot see. We have walked into a place of transition. Although we have asked, we are unprepared to receive. Transition is for prepared people! When you stay focused, transition will take place and it will be good.

Have you ever driven down a street unaware that a parade was going on? The traffic is backed up. Pedestrians have the right of way to walk in front of your car every time there is an opportunity for you to inch forward. You might become frustrated and start screaming for the people to move out of the way because you have somewhere to go, and the parade has already made you late.

What I have found is that in the midst of what looks like chaos and confusion is really your answered prayer. You just have not realized that God has sent this parade to bring you what you've been asking for. At first, everything in the parade sounds so noisy. But if you just slow down and relax, everything will fall into place. You then will begin to hear the music that was playing the entire time—a beautiful melody of cascading sounds filling the atmosphere. It's almost soothing if you could stop yelling at the children in the backseat who are continuously fighting. The band procession marches past. Their costumes are artistically designed with handmade accessories. The colors are bold and eye catching to provoke roaring cheers from the crowd that lines the streets. *How unique*, you think to yourself. At last, the floats begin their way down the street. They are the most creative things you have ever seen. You are so close you can even see the minute details of the decorations. A peace finally settles over you. The last float passes by and soon after the traffic begins to flow again. Then, you say, *It's about time! They are always doing something to slow me down.* As the way opens up, you speed off to your destination.

You have just missed your moment of opportunity. We do not seem to understand the way God operates. He does not move the way we move or even think the way we think. Have you ever thought about creating a universe? That's my point. His ideas are so vast that if He did not feed us the crumbs from His cookie, our minds would overload and burst. Think about this. When we have too much stuff weighing on us at one time, we get stress headaches, muscle tension, strokes, heart attacks, etc. Because our minds are not equipped to handle all of it, our bodies are impacted. If a full thought of God came in, it would kill you. This is why He gives us information in pieces and as needed. Those of you who already walk in the spirit know the weight of a thought of God. He has to come in and carry the load for you just so that you can contain the thought.

So, if this is true, and it is, why do we continue to lose out or become stagnant? Because you have failed to positioned yourself for transition. You have not noticed that things have changed. Colors are brighter and sounds are peaceful. Until you can recognize where you are now at, you cannot walk into the blessings that are all around you. Without a change of mind, you will never walk into new victories. Stop praying to hit the lottery. Stop looking for the drug dealer to drop a bag of money in your backyard. And don't look for your mate to die so that you can collect life insurance, Social Security, or any other inheritance that you would be entitled to. You have done yourself a disservice if you receive any of these things and still have the same mindset. You will not prosper and have good success!

Your prosperity is in your transitioning to another level of wisdom and understanding. Inheritance is good, but if you only know how to spend it, it will be your curse and not your blessing. Ultimately, it will leave you in a worse emotional state than when you first began.

I have written about a lot of controversial circumstances I have travailed through. It almost seems gossipy. This was not an easy task put before me. To be open like this comes from a very mature place. It is a place I stand in with God and for God. He is my strength.

I have done things that are not suitable for dinner table discussions. I don't regret where I have been. I do regret some of the things that I have done. If I could go back and change them, I would. I have to be honest. When I was out there in my sins, I enjoyed it. Sin was fun. It was fun as I knew fun to be at that time. Life had offered me a bowl of cherries, and I ate the whole fruit, even the pits. No one told me that I was not supposed to eat the whole thing. Opportunity was before me and I ate a never-filling portion. I was always looking for something that would hit the spot and then I would be satisfied, I thought! It never happened. I lived in a place of never-ending confusion, and despair was the result. With little hope to dream and no vision on the horizon, fear was the best emotion I could conjure up. Anger and frustration was how fear demonstrated itself in my life. "Where there is no vision, the people parish:" (Proverbs 29:18).

It is my belief that this book will prompt change for somebody looking for a change. You may not fully understand what it is you are seeking or what needs to change, but you know something has to. As you continue to read, set your mind on change. The more you focus on it the quicker change will come. It will require work, but there is hope in a life lifted up out of the marred clay. And, marred clay is what we are. God is truly a healer. He can turn an ugly duckling into a beautiful black swan. He is an awesome Creator! He knows where you are and just what to do. I can only tell you what I know about Him, but my true desire is for you to know Him in a personal and intimate way. He knows how to fill you up until there is no space for loneliness, doubt, fear, hatred, hurt, anger, or any other negative emotion. He will pour so much love into you that it will pour out of you onto everyone else. We have taken all of these other poisonous venoms and saturated the environment we occupy; why not love? It really is what you have been looking for, and you can't get that from another person. In the center of your belly is a resting place. It longs to be filled. It is the focal point of the spirit man.

Have you noticed that whatever emotions you feel rest in the pit of your belly? Good or bad, they all come from the same place. It is a place that God has created for Himself. No matter what you do or who you do it with, that space can only be filled by Him. If you ever come to understand and embrace that, you are already halfway through your process. Just remember that you have to invite Him in and admit that you need Him. People may care about what you have done and who you have done it with, but my God still loves no matter what you have done in life. He loves you as if you had done nothing at all. That's awesome to me!

God is looking for the one who will just believe Him. Believe Him, believe His Word, and you will see mighty works that you can't even imagine. I encourage you to take a moment right now to reflect on where you are in your life and where you want to be. Are you in a place of inner peace that cannot be stolen tomorrow? Is your life fulfilled to completeness? Are you ready for a change? What is the cost to you changing or not changing? In order to endure, you must know what you are willing to give up. Don't get to the end of your life with regrets from today. You can get to the end of your life completely fulfilled and with no regrets. That's what I want for you.

You are one step away from obtaining freedom from all that ails you. If you're thinking, *I'm not a prisoner to anyone or anything; I am free*, my question is, are you sure? Any thought, feeling, or action that can cause you to respond against truth (not facts because facts can fail you) could cause you to be a prisoner. Your prison walls may have gone up in your childhood. Maybe it was from a bad relationship or marriage or from a current or past abuse. Know that freedom is only as far away as making a decision. You just need to choose to be free. Do you want the chains loosed from you? Chains can get heavy over time. When you carry them day after day, they weigh you down and change your normal posture. Eventually, you will become hunched over. No one wants to be hunched over. Choose to lose the weight.

When you get through with alcohol and drug use, mental health issues, unwanted pregnancies, fornication and adultery, unstable parenting techniques, lying, cheating, and a mass of other possible complicated circumstances, there is still hope. Sometimes we inherit a mentality that is not conducive to our future success. Remember, our mentality could be passed on from generation to generation. It is even sometimes referred to as a "bad seed" that keeps being passed along. Or some might say, "It seems to be in the blood." No matter how many generations it fell in, you have the power to stop it. It only takes one person to stand up and say, "Enough is enough! This will not continue on my watch." Our children will learn by what they see. Show them the way to freedom. Speak it; live it; and pass it on. The blood of Jesus changes everything. It is all you need. Accept Jesus as your Lord and Savior and change will come.

The process of my transition involved seeing things as they really were in my life. I had to look at myself and others' intentions toward me. I found that most people's intentions toward me were not good. I only saw this when I decided to be completely honest with myself. It was not easy, but it was necessary. Many times when I went to my mom, she would not give me advice. She would just say, "Experience is necessary." I was usually looking for someone to get on board with me. It never happened. When things get uncomfortable in life, we always try to find people who will wallow in the mud with us. It helps us to feel better about our circumstances. You know the saying: birds of a feather flock together.

As I ventured on, I still had many dark moments. I found myself writing these words in my journal:

> Over the years, so many people have spoken negativity into my life. They expected me to fail. I did not realize the impact that it has had on my mind and spirit. I always wondered why I would start so many things. In the midst of it becoming successful, I would suddenly change course. Then I could not understand why it had failed.

> I take full responsibility for where I am today. How I got here is a story of dream quenchers, destiny destroyers, and prey devourers. They are people who had been in my life and meant

well. Due to their own issues of low self-esteem, insecurities, and incompetency in their own abilities, they projected their negativity onto me. They found that it was easier to discourage others from accomplishing what they would not dare to embark upon or even dream.

I am starting to realize that most of the people who have been assigned to my life have been sent to stop me from accomplishing my God-given destiny. (God has everything already planned for your life. As I have already told you, the enemy does too. I was assigned to my mother because God knew she would protect the destiny that lay inside of me. She would help to push me toward my divine path.) When I consider the magnitudes of people who have come to hold me back, I know that my future has to be greater than I could ever imagine.

I see now that I need to press forward. A subtle word of discouragement kills a roaring fire of dreams over time. I now realize that the only thing left is what others have imparted in you. After weathering the storm for so long, it is hard to start a fire with wet wood. I need God to come in and dry up all the water that has been left from the storm. The sun is shining, but the land is drenched. The seeds are there. They were planted way before the storm reared its ugly face. Some were washed away. Others are planted so deeply that the same rain that came to destroy the land so that crops will not grow will ultimately give life and strong roots to those seeds. These seeds the destroyer did not even know were there.

I see those seeds taking root deep below the surface. Deeper and deeper the roots are stretching downward. Because of the trampling under heavy feet, it has been pressed firmly into place. Everyone forgot that the seed was there; even the ground that it was planted in has forgotten about the lost seeds.

As the sun drives away the water, something is about to happen. The form of the seed has changed. It is grounded and rooted deeply. It's reaching toward its purpose. It is positioned right at the surface of the soil waiting for one final push upward. The final breakthrough is here. As the head of the plant reaches toward the sun, it shouts to its destiny, "Wait for me. I made it through and I am on my way up!"

Life is not always fair. It does not always play nice. It can pull on the very being of your soul. Sometimes things are too big for little ones to bear. Some disappointments seem small, but when you are already on overload, it will tip the scales. At these times, seek God because He is near. Just trust in Him. He will bring forth a hope of faith that changes destinies. He will change you, and you can become a world changer.

Life will develop you. You may become stagnant. It could even kill you mentally, physically, or spiritually. But, you still have the power in your hands to cause directions to change. No matter how old you are, it's never too late to start reaching for change.

I want you to take a moment to assess the fullness of your life. You don't have to strive to be better than anyone else. Strive to be the best *you* that you can be. There is no one like you. God made only one. You are uniquely designed to do only what you can do. So rejoice in being the only you. We are here but for a little while. Consider that when you get to the end of this life and it's your time to die, don't just close your eyes and die. Don't die with your hurts, pains, regrets, and hopes and dreams still inside you, but die healed and fulfill all of your dreams. Let others say, "It was a life well spent." You deserve it!

CHAPTER 11

Riches from Glory

As time went on, my life changed dramatically. I had been blessed to have four sons. All of them were healthy for the most part. God's plan for my life was unfolding. It was not, and still is not, without its daily challenges. Every day presents new opportunities to embark upon the grace of God. And trust me; I need it. My salvation and peace is everything to me. This walk has been one of the toughest roads I have travelled yet. It is also the most fulfilling. My commitment is not hard to fulfill. Going against my flesh in the struggle can be tedious. This journey truly isn't about the end reward of material achievements or successes. It's about the treasured items that are in the lessons learned along the way. Sometimes we are so focused on the destination that we miss our own party, a party sponsored by God Himself.

Life is like a collage with snapshots of life experiences, dreams, and visions of the future. In close proximity, you see small, individual snapshots. If you stand far enough back, the photos appear to be knitted together and form a beautiful scenic picture. Perspective really is everything. It changes the view.

We are not capable of seeing the whole picture. We would have to have the ability to see into our own future. Through

God eyes, we can see properly. Please don't misunderstand me! I am not talking about psychics or any other telepathic source. I have been there too. It really will take you further than you want to go, stay longer than you want to stay, and pay a price that you cannot pay. Do not dabble in the world of psychics, palm readers, mediums, or witchcraft. They do have powers that should not be taken lightly. In addition, don't participate in candle lighting, incense, altars, or offerings of any sort to these spirits. It is an abomination to the Almighty God. Trust me; you don't want to open those doors. He is the only One Who has true power to destroy the enemy's works. It takes the power of God to pull down these strongholds. You will never be free until you are free from this behavior and the impact that it has had on your life and your children's lives. It affects your life and everything connected to you. What seems like innocent child's play at one point will turn serious if you ever try to get away from it. The demonic forces that I spoke about fighting earlier were due to me opening these same doors. As my mother always said, experience is necessary. I never liked it or understood it when she spoke it. Now, I understand exactly what she was saying. You must go through some things in order to grow to maturity. The key is to learn from your experiences. I learned about these forces. You will ultimately reap destruction if you sow into that world. I know that this is of the devil, and it is bondage.

You may still be a skeptic of this information that I presented to you. I was too for a long time. I learned the hard way. I found myself deeply involved with all of these things. I was taking my friends and family to hell with me by introducing them to this activity. I, once again, thank my God for having a plan for my life. It was only Him who stepped in and pulled me out.

The devil cannot contend with God. He can contend with the angels because he is an angel. He is an angel of darkness and evil. It is his one job to get every human being he can to follow him. He knows that God the Father has given power to man, even the power to overrule demonic forces, in Jesus' name.

He wants you to believe his lies through your thoughts; then he can pull you away from the truth of who you are. That's where he plants his seeds of thoughts—in your mind. You think you are forming these perverted thoughts and evil acts that pop up in your mind. They are not from you. They are from him. He then uses shame, guilt, and fear of anyone finding out about the hundreds of negative thoughts that run through your mind. When you don't have the knowledge or power to defeat him in his game, you will ultimately succumb to the thoughts that have now turned into desires in your heart. You might think that it is just the way you are. It's not. It's what you have become through your path of thinking. The Bible says that as a man thinks in his heart, so he will become (Proverbs 23:7). The thoughts come. You then embrace the thoughts. They rest in your heart and become your desire. All of the desires planted by the devil will lead to death. It seems well, but you will eventually die spiritually and possibly physically.

There is a place called hell and it is real. Just as heaven is real. You have heard the stories. If you haven't, let me tell you. Hell is a real place, and it is not on this earth. It is a place that God had to create that at the appointed time, the devil and all his partakers will be exiled to. Your worst day put together with everyone else's worst day still won't measure up to the pain and torture that you will suffer in hell. Hell was never created for you; God's plan was not for man to be destined to that eternal place. You end up there by choice. Either you will choose life of death. If I am wrong, I have lived my life in peace and showing love to those whose path I cross. If I am right, I avoid hell, and great is my reward with God. Either way I win, and hell is not worth the risk of being unsure. So what happens if you are wrong and hell is real? After you die, there is no compromising or asking for forgiveness. The decision you make today (tomorrow is not promised) will decide where you will be later.

The Bible says, "The thief (devil) cometh not, but for to steal, and to kill, and to destroy: I am come that they might have life, and that they might have it more abundantly" (John 10:10). It is God who has come to give you an abundant life through Jesus the Messiah (the anointed One). God has the power to destroy yokes of bondage. Spiritual warfare is when you decide that you want to go in a different direction than what the devil has offered you. He then comes with his power. He will cause so much to happen in your life that you will want to change your mind and turn back just to stop the war. If he knows you are trying to get out of his grip, he will try to kill you, literally.

So where is God in all of this? He's right there waiting for you to call on Him. He's not like the devil. He will not force Himself on you. He's a gentleman. I have found out that all I need to do is say, "God no matter what I go through, I trust You." God always prevails! God doesn't always cause your troubles to leave at once. Sometimes He will allow them to slowly change. As I said before, God has given power the man. When you stick with the process, you will learn to fight the devil yourself in the power of God. If God did it all for you, you would learn nothing. And then how will you be able to teach someone else?

I have heard that you can be pitiful or powerful, but you can't be both. When you bow down to the devil and his tactics, you are pitiful. God wants you powerful. Everything that I have spoken about in this book, I have lived and learned. Through these experiences, a warrior has begun to emerge.

I now stand on an unshakable foundation. I received all of this through God, not man. No book knowledge here. I don't knock school, but it will not teach you the revelation of God. That only comes through the Spirit of God. We all have things we are working on to better ourselves. To do that, we must empty ourselves completely out. Your past must no longer have a stronghold on you. You will then become so full of your future that the real you will emerge, and you will become whole in your spirit. Just remember when you empty out the dead things you must be refilled with life. This is the life of the Spirit, which comes from God Himself.

When you are really ready for change, invite Jesus in. It's a simple prayer that changes everything.

> **Jesus I need You. Come into my heart and change me. I am asking You to be Lord and Savior over my life. I am sorry for all that I have done. Forgive me. I know that You are the Son of God. You came into the earth to die for me. Now I am in the right place with the Father. It is in Your name, Jesus, that I pray. Amen.**

CHAPTER 12

A Warrior Emerging

In the beginning, God created male and female. He created them both in one being. Their name was Adam. The creature called "man" that God made in His own likeness was longing for companionship with a fellow species like himself. Being the Great Creator, the all-wise and knowing God, He placed His "man" into a deep sleep. He opened up his side, took a rib out, and closed him back up. He let him rest until he was fully restored from the transformation that had taken place.

You see, when God breathed life into man, He put lives into him. The Bible does not say He had to breathe life into this second Adam (Eve) all over again. The life was already in the creation. It was in the bone and everything else He used to complete her process. The fact that God was in it tells me that the life was already there because God *is* life. When God took the rib, He left Adam number one with a male spirit. God had given a command and told them from the beginning that they were to have dominion, take authority, and resupply all of the land and subdue everything that was in it. That included all the spiritual forces that would have access to this earth that God gave to them.

Eve was Adam's counterpart. She was the completion of God's process of man. She must have been special. God set her aside until the work of her mansion and her garden was completely decorated with flowers, diamonds, emeralds, rubies, gold, and other precious stones. The food in the Garden was magnificent, and the air was always filled with sweet fragrances. Everything there was perfect, and she spent every day with God. She was beautiful and lacked nothing. The food even kept her youthful and strong. It kept her skin toned and blemish free. What more could a girl ask for?

When she was created, she lacked nothing! God decided it was time to reward His first man Adam with His prize possession, Eve. God led her right across his path. I can imagine that when Adam saw her, he said, "My, my, my, that's my bone and my flesh." He knew that God had done something special for him. His eyes had not seen, his ears had not heard, neither had it even entered into his spirit what God was going to bless him with (1 Corinthians 2:9). She was God's signature piece, and Adam knew she belonged to him.

Eve knew she had it going on! She was whole and complete. She lacked nothing and was full in all things. Eve knew who she was. After spending so much time with God, how could she not know who she was? That was a given.

When deception crept in, it began with a word, a thought, and a promise that distracted her. Distractions can cost you your life. Your life is a big price to pay. We have a choice as to whether or not we entertain the thoughts that come into our minds. Have you ever heard the saying, "An idle mind is the devil's workshop"? This is saying that if you don't keep your mind occupied with positive thoughts, it allows time and space for negative thoughts to be created and take over. Ultimately, they will overtake you. Just know that they are sent to distract you. The thoughts that occupy your mind will have a hold on our life. If you want to understand why you are where you are, take an account of your daily thoughts and whatever is ruling in them is the outcome of what you are living.

Eve discussed these things with the first man, and a decision was made. They went against what they had already known. This usually happens when you start to second guessing what you know. You know that's not what your parents taught you. But you do it anyway. Then afterward, you say, "I knew better than that. Why did I do that?" This clears up the long discussion that we could have about why Eve disobeyed God. We all know that we have been paying the price ever since. We are also paying the price for the choices we have made in our own lives.

Moving forward two thousand or so years, we have Jesus that comes on the scene. He is the promise that had been spoken of since the first two Adams messed up. God said He would send the seed of a woman. He was the second Adam set and sent. Remember I told you Eve was the completed original version. God said it would be what comes out of her that would set things back in motion to His original plan. God said she would crush the head of the thing that deceived her through what would be living inside for her. The head is symbolic of the power source. Therefore, she would take back the power that was stolen from the beginning.

The deceiver is that enemy I told you about earlier. He's the one that started this whole mess, not the woman. She did fall into his trap, and it was a deadly one. God don't make faulty product. That's how I know that she fell victim to his scheme. Now, this is really cool. God goes right back to the beginning and says, "I gave you authority over this place that I put you in. I am not a liar. If I said it, then that's what it is." He uses the same instrument (Eve, woman) that was victimized and said, "You will take authority over that thing that caused you to fall. What you are carrying inside of you will be the redemption for your wrongdoing." He is the only way! Redemption means to be brought back, to be put back into place. That means you have the authority that was given to the first Adams. The only special requirement is Jesus. He is that Seed and the Son that is able to redeem you. He's the One I told you about before. Go back and read it if you need to. It's up to you what you do with this new but rightful position once you have been placed in it. No one can take this place for you. Either you will continue to give away your power, as was done from the beginning, or you will stand up and take your rightful place. The choice is yours.

Do you really understand who you are? You have given your power over to the world and still wonder why the manifestations of your heart's desires have not sprung forth. If you really understood, you would no longer give yourself to friends who continually mistreat you, family members who take your kindness for weakness, and men who say they love you but don't see you as good enough to marry. The question is, do you think you are good enough to marry or just good enough to lay with? I need to be direct with you because we are at the end of this book, and you may still think that I am talking to someone else. I know sometimes we sell ourselves the lie that we don't want to get married. The truth is in that midnight hour when you are there alone. What is the truth behind the pain and anger of your brokenness? The pain of the past will subside, but truth still comes forth. Being married does not eliminate you from these questions. If the truth be told, many married women thought marriage was the soothing balm to their wounds. They are finding out it's not! Your man cannot heal you. For the woman who is hiding from relationships all together, it's not that you don't trust them; you don't trust yourself or God. You don't trust that you will be able to discern if his intentions are as they seem. After making the same mistake time and time again, fear of the pain causes you to pull totally back and that's safe. The sad and funny thing about it all is you justify your own mistreatment and continually promote it. There is a lot more to say about this, but I'll leave that alone.

We were created to be counterparts. Does that mean that we cannot be happy alone? Absolutely not! We should be happy and complete with or without a mate. What I am saying is that there is another part of us that is waiting to be linked to another. We were never made to be alone forever. I do believe that a man's heart will always wander until he finds his Eve, and a woman's heart will always wander until she finds her Adam. It's not my opinion. It's God's opinion.

Sometimes we find comfort in having a title or position. It still does not account for who you are. There comes a time when titles no longer matter. The world makes gestures to identify who you are by giving you a title. It represents your value to society. We wear the hats of a husband or wife, mom or dad, sister or brother, as well as our job titles . . . or should we call them labels? It's your choice; it's all the same. We identify ourselves as police officers, firefighters, soldiers, doctors, lawyers, teachers, or even preachers. I could go on, but I think you get my point. We are all of those things, but we are so much more. Although these titles may be factual, they are not the core of who you are. If this is what you identify with, then what happens when the title or label is gone?

You are building your foundation on sinking sand. The house will eventually collapse. These positions are only held for an appointed amount of time. If this is what makes you who you are, your very being is temporal. I have seen the foundations of strong men and women crumble, and you have also. Whether it is a family member, a coworker, or celebrity, it is devastating to witness. There is so much more to you than a title. I hope you know that. If not, please take my advice and find out. It takes more than a day, week, or even a month. It could take years. It depends on how much stuff you have to sift through to get to the foundation and how willing you are to be real with yourself. After the process, you will know.

A solid foundation is what you need. When a house is built upon a rock, it may shift a little, but it will not fall. It will adjust and settle during changes in weather, atmosphere, and environmental issues. Overtime, some pieces may fall off and need to be replaced, but the house will last. A solid foundation is found in your purpose, and purpose can be found in your passion. Your passion will be your pillars in tough times. This life is bigger than we are. Your passion will connect you to the fulfillment of inner peace and true happiness. I believe it is all linked to God's plan for you. Along the way, you will identify who you are.

This world can take away your title, but it cannot take the true identity of who you are. It is as unchanging as a solid rock. In an ever-changing world, it's good to know that some things are constant. For me, it's my God. I have found that my hope in Him has kept me stable in the toughest of times. He has been consistent with His words, His hand, and His face. He cannot and will not ever fail you or me in His plan for our lives. I trust Him and I hope you do as well.

As we desire to have relationships with others, we have got to know who we are and what we want. God does not change relationships; He changes the people in the relationship. It is still a choice that must be made by individuals. If you are looking for God to change your situation, pray that He may change you and then the other person's heart toward you. As in any relationship, you must be in agreement with each other on major issues. Relationships are hard work. It is even harder work when you are not in agreement, or if one or both of you have not been through the process of healing.

In the midst of all of this, we try to find happiness together. It does not matter who you are with; they will not be able to make you happy. Happiness comes from within. No one can give it to you. They can only share in what you already have. If you can understand this concept, you will save yourself a whole lot of heartache, and it will release your partner from the responsibility of making you happy. He or she is not your answer; God is your answer. He is the only One Who can develop and complete you. If you are not in a relationship yet and you are honest enough with yourself to know that you are not happy with you, don't seek to be with anyone else. Go through the healing process and then allow someone to come in. The thing you get healed from will not be allowed to take up residence in your life ever again. You will have done yourself and your mate a favor.

What is the thing that has caused you to get off the path to your destiny? You have been commanded to take control of it. If you are a child of God the Father, you have received Jesus as your covering. If Jesus is your covering, then healing, health, wisdom, wealth, and victory is yours. Your destiny is in knowing who you are. This life is a journey, but it's a road worth taking. Don't be afraid to be different and stand out in a crowd. I dare you to be different! That is what will make you greater. As I have said and showed, God has a perfect plan for all of our lives. It is bigger than you could ever imagine. Early in my walk, I had a very small vision for my future. I could not see past the goal of having all of my bills paid and a ten thousand dollar surplus in the bank. I have prayed for God to give me a vision and a plan for my life. I needed to see farther and dream bigger for myself. Before you can be it, you must see it. Dreams do come true. Because of God, I see more than I ever have. He continues to increase my thinking more and more each day. As He encourages me, I will pour it back out and encourage you. We will live together, love together, heal together, and prosper with purpose.

This is just the closing of a chapter that has laid the foundation for the next chapter in my life. It is an opportunity for new growth and experiences. New beginnings are what I have been pressing toward. This focus is what strengthens me in times of trouble. Life truly is like a book. As we flip through the pages, information is shared and received, and change could take place due to the impact of the content. When we get to the end of that chapter, nothing else is written until the new chapter begins. The rest of the page is left blank until the page is turned. The previous chapters are done. Once the page is turned, the only way to see what was written is to flip backward through the pages.

I have stepped out of the darkness of pain, hurt, rejection, abuse, abandonment, loneliness, insufficiencies, and insecurities. I've stepped into the light of a new dimension of hopes, dreams, peace, true love, prosperity, joy, health, healing, and oneness with the Father and the Son, Who is the light of this world. I am so excited about what is coming into my life. My future is much brighter than my past. I know that the God I serve loves me. I am so special to Him that He etched out a plan for my life well before my beginning. He has taught me to love myself and others. No offense is so great that it is worth your inheritance or your salvation. Remember that forgiveness is the gift that you give to yourself.

I have seen more hypocrisy in the church than in the world. Don't let church folk trip you up and cause you to leave your solid foundation. The only person who will pay the price is you. And the cost is great. Persecution has come on every hand and from directions that I would have never expected. The offenses against me were great enough to cause me to leave the Body of Christ altogether. Twelve years is a long time to leave home. This is why we must be God focused and not man focused. If God is all that matters, you will not be moved because of an emotion. What we feel, think, and say can get us going in a direction that is hazardous to us. Don't blow your own smoke and clog your own way. Stay on the straight road and stay focused. It will take you far in the journey.

God has given me the opportunity to come back and commune with Him. I learned that I had committed myself to the church, but not to God Himself. Did I not say that He was the One Who called me? Men will fail you in and out of the church, but if you are committed to God, you can sit, walk, or stand through any adversity. You will be able to teach those around you something they don't understand— with God, I can do all things (Philippians 4:13). You will be able to say, "No one and no situation can determine my outcome. I am no longer what was. I am what is to be, and God is in it all, for my life is hidden in Him." The Bible says that when I see Jesus as He is, I will be like Him. As He is, I am (3 John 3:2).

In my fall, my eyes were on man; in my conversion, my eyes were on Jesus the Christ, my Lord and Savior. He is the One Who has left a road map for me to follow. With that in place, I don't need any other thing for my journey. Everything is on the road. I just have to arrive at the provision. Too many times we get off the road just before we reach the point where things change. It's not easy when you can't see what's up ahead. But I encourage you to press on. Your breakthrough is just around the bend!

God has given me beauty for the ashes that were left from what was placed upon my altar. The ashes are what are left from the fires that consume the offering. God has given me a garment of praise that I wear everywhere I go. These garments were received from the tears that were cried in the midnight hours of life. God has strengthened me to be an overcomer in every situation, and He has crowned me with His righteousness for my submission. God loves me, but He loves you the same. What He is doing in my life, He wants to do in yours as well. He wants to do even greater. He says just believe and the things that you are believing for will happen (Mark 11:23). I pray that God blesses all of you. I know you will be great and do great things! I'll see you on the other side when we emerge as warriors in "The Dawning of a New Day!"

Who Is She? She Is a Woman!

She is a warrior emerging. Every day that she awakes and her feet touch the floor, the enemy hears the thunderous roar of her footsteps. They cause him to freeze. Her footsteps are as the steps of God. It confuses the devil, and he does not know the difference in the sound. He sees a blood-covered offering. The offering has been accepted by God. Therefore, trouble has come to knock at his door. She is dripping with blood from head to toe, as he trembles in fear standing before her. He knows that the battle is already won and he is defeated. As she advances forward from out of that hidden place in God, the shadows of darkness fade as the light of glory shines upon her face. She is a beautiful creature that has been uniquely created high above the heavens. She has been through a birthing process like no other.

She is a warrior! She stands tall and strong. She is fierce and feminine. The spirit within her eyes will cut even to the soul. She has chosen to take the high road as she comes out of the valley. As she mounts up on wings as eagles, she runs the race and soars above the storms. It is in the midst of the storm where she gets her strength, and the winds propel her forward and higher. She has learned how to lighten her load so that life no longer weighs her down. She will not die in a battle nor get stuck in your storm. She radiates confidence because she knows that she is victorious through Jesus the Messiah. He is the anointed One and has come to anoint her. She cannot be stopped and is prepared to eradicate anything that stands in her way. She carries a sword in her hand and a weapon in her mouth that will assassinate her enemies near and far. Her gestures are flamboyantly graceful. Her every move is strategically controlled. She is truly a force to be reckoned with. Just as the flowers of the field are gently blown with the winds of heaven, so is she.

Every warrior must learn to wait patiently. It is in the waiting that necessary skills are developed. These skills are learned so she can ambush the enemy because he must be utterly destroyed. With every stripe of war paint she wears, it represents her victories won in the battles. She no longer compromises the gifts that have been given to her. She is uniquely designed, and her schematic cannot be copied. Her presence radiates the glory of the kingdom of God, and her faith is not optional. God has highly favored her openly. The world sees it and the enemy knows it.

So, to the onlookers who ask who I am—I am a woman! I am a warrior emerging. I have a destiny to fulfill and a purpose that awaits me. It has already been written, and those words go before me. The words that others have thrown at me like rocks, I have used as stepping-stones. I am thankful for them. It has built me a stairwell to walk out of my pit and into the palace that was already mine. I just happened to lose sight of it before it was in full view. But now, I walk in the power and authority of the Holy Ghost. I wear a crown of royalty. In it are laid stones of precious purple zeal. I have been crowned with wisdom, knowledge, and understanding, which I received from my Father the King. The world can never steal it, and it shall never be taken away from me. Why? Because it was not given to me by man but by Father God. So I take my place in His kingdom and my authority in this world. Rest assured that the fight is not over. There is much more to come. I have overcome this world as King Jesus has. So come what may, I will stand strong and I will win! Thank You, my dear heart, my Husband, my Friend, my King, my God. I will wear this crown forever. Amen.

> "We are stronger than you think, weaker than you know, wiser than we appear, and more powerful than you could ever imagine."
>
> —The Women's Group of New England (TWGNE)

"I have fought a good fight,
I have finished my course,
I have kept the faith:
Henceforth there is laid up for me
a crown of righteousness, which the Lord,
the righteous judge, shall give me at that
day: and not to me only, but unto all them
also that love his appearing"
(2 Timothy 4:7–8).

CPSIA information can be obtained
at www.ICGtesting.com
Printed in the USA
FFOW04n1855231014
8304FF

9 781613 142370